TRADING SYSTEM ANALYSIS

Using Trading Simulations
and Generated Data to Test,
Evaluate and Predict Trading
System Performance

TRADING SYSTEM ANALYSIS

Using Trading Simulations
and Generated Data to Test,
Evaluate and Predict Trading
System Performance

ROBERT M. BARNES

McGraw-Hill

New York   San Francisco   Washington, D.C.   Auckland   Bogotá
Caracas   Lisbon   London   Madrid   Mexico City   Milan
Montreal   New Dehli   San Juan   Singapore
Sydney   Tokyo   Toronto

Library of Congress Cataloging-in-Publication Data

Barnes, Robert M.
    Trading system analysis: using trading simulations and generated data to test,
  evaluate and predict trading system performance / Robert M. Barnes
      p. cm.
    Includes index.
    ISBN 0-7863-1098-7
    1. Commodity exchanges—Computer simulation. 2. Stocks—Computer
  simulation.   I. Title.
  HG046.B342 1997
  332.64'01'13—dc21   96–53447

McGraw-Hill
A Division of The McGraw·Hill Companies

1 2 3 4 5 6 7 8 9 0 DOC/DOC 9 0 9 8 7

ISBN 0-7863-1098-7

Printed and bound by R. R. Donnelley & Sons Company.

This publication is designed to provide accurate and authoritative information in regard to the
subject matter covered. It is sold with the understanding that neither the author nor the publisher is
engaged in rendering legal, accounting, or other professional service. If legal advice or other
expert assistance is required, the services of a competent professional person should be sought.

> *—From a Declaration of Principles jointly adopted by a Committee*
> *of the American Bar Association and a Committee of Publishers.*

McGraw-Hill books are available at special quantity discounts to use as premiums and sales
promotions, or for use in corporate training programs. For more information, please write to the
Director of Special Sales, McGraw-Hill, 11 West 19th Street, New York, NY 10011. Or contact
your local bookstore.

To my family,
Laura, Bryan, and Jeffrey,
for their wonderful love and support.

Even before the advent of fast computers to speed up vast numbers of calculations, traders had arduously tested their trading plans to find out how profitable they would be. From using simple lines drawn on price charts and arriving at casual conslusions about profits and losses, to performing meticulous accounting of position entry and exit and mixing of different instruments, these earlier traders sought to understand what made the markets tick and their portfolios profit. Computers came along and allowed traders and analysts vast and intensive calculations for many methods and instrument alternatives.

But the bottom line has always been the same: Test a trading method over a piece of history and analyze/categorize the results, but expect much of the same profit/loss results for the future. Some variants followed, such as using more sophisticated (statistical) analytical techniques like hypothesis testing and in-sample/out-of-sample (no hindsight) data, but the *results* of simulating trading performance have been much the same: future real-time trading results do not match the simulated trading performances.

The need is still there: Traders want to know how their methods will perform in the future. Unfortunately, current trade simulation techniques have not answered that question. Even excellent real-time trading results have not continued into the future. Traders still want some way of testing their methods' effectiveness and want to come away with a high degree of confidence with simulated projections. Traders need good representations of the future, simulation methods and analysis techniques, to be able to draw accurate conclusions about how their methods will fare.

We do have good statistical methodologies and fast computers. What traders lack now are good representations of future scenarios.

This book delves into simulations, trading methods, price behavior, and endeavors to build truer price scenarios for testing purposes. If we can provide the trader with good, plentiful price situations, he can use the already-adequate statistical and simulation trchniques and come up with accurate trade result projections.

The first chapter discusses and refines the various components of a total trading system. The trader must be concerned about risk—how to measure and control it; trading candidate selection; timing of buying and selling; and portfolio management.

Next, we discuss the general idea of simulation, the concept and purpose of mimicking and projecting performance of a trading system and of general systems. Real-time trading is compared with simulation methodology.

Our next inquiry goes into the inner workings of trading simulations and price models. Price behavior in general is discussed. We delve into scenario possibilities arising out of price move magnitudes, probabilities, and orderings over time. These combinations tell the trader how price movements/patterns could happen. Finally, price behavior models are brought into the portfolio plan and related to profits.

A very central Chapter 4 examines in great detail how price scenarios are generated, starting with the choice of past periods to model and including time considerations and price characteristics to incorporate. Considerable attention is paid to three particular price models; the random walk, sequential walk, and price vector models as representing the span form academic- to trader-oriented models. Procedures for calculation and use are given, along with many examples of these three models in different markets, and are contrasted with each other in the same market with one instrument.

Chapter 5 outlines and details the main components of a complete trading system, from risk and initial capital considerations to real-time trading and portfolio administration. The central engine, research and development, drives the profit-seeking system: If trading methods are properly researched and applied to viable future scenarios, profits result.

In the future traders will search more carefully the past for periods to best represent the future, not exactly (as history will not repeat in a rigid, step-by-step pattern), but in a general fashion. They will generate, using simulations like mine, many really possible scenarios using the best representation from the past.

New developments in simulation methodology should include search technologies to find tell-tale signs of the best historical periods to use for building future scenarios. This will involve developing good mathematical methods for determining probabilities of new scenarios and better forecasting tools for simple price projections to complex price patterns. However, in tandem to new mathematical work, there will be increased reliance on expert trader judgment to choose best representative historical periods as input to the simulation models.

Robert M. Barnes

CONTENTS

List of Figures   xv
List of Tables   xvi
List of Charts   xvii

Chapter 1

Systematic Trading   1

Risk Management   1
    Personal Risk Attitude   2
    Measuring/Evaluating Risk: Some Indicators   2
    A New Return/Risk Index   6
Selection of Trading Candidates   7
Timing Methods   9
Portfolio Management   11
    Initial and Reinvestment Monies   11
    Other Administrative Steps   12
    Running the Daily Operation   12
    Discipline   14

Chapter 2

Actual versus Simulated Trading Results   19

Good Simulations, Bad Results   20
Real Traders in Live Times   21
Current Simulation Usage   23
About Simulations in General   26

Chapter 3

Realistic Trading Simulations   33

Price Movements: A Short Course   34
Scenario Possibilities   36
Scenario Probabilities and Price Simulation Planning   40
Basic Combinations: Price Change Ordering and Magnitudes   40
Price Models   42
Model Test Design   43
Overall Portfolio Plan   45

Chapter 4

Price Scenario Generation   47

Choosing Past Periods   47
   Time Considerations   49
   Price Characteristics   49
Choosing Price Models   56
Examples of Three Models   58
   The Random Walk Model   58
   The Sequential Walk Model   62
   The Price Vector Model   64
      Data Collection for the Price Vector Model   66
      Constructing Price Vectors   68
Examples of Price Models   70
Generation of Price Data   89
   Examples of Generated Data   91
Different Markets   91
   Sideways Markets   91
   Uptrend Markets   111
   Downtrend Markets   111
   The Different Market Price Change Distributions   121
Different Models   124
   Three Models at Work   125
      The Random Walk Model in Action   125
      The Sequential Walk Model Applied   128
      The Price Vector Model at Work   133

Chapter 5

The Complete Trading System   145

The Complete Trading System   146

The Monies Management System   148

Return/Risk Categorization and Assignment   148

Risk Control   150

Determining Initial Capital   151

Calculating Number of Instruments   151

The Selection Management System   152

The Research and Development System   154

The Portfolio Administration System   156

Summary/Examples   159

Index   163

1–1   Measuring Risk: Drawdowns in a Portfolio   6
1–2   Investment Speedometer   8
2–1   Historical Tests and Real-Time Trading with the Moving
       Average Method   21
2–2   Simulation Testing Approaches   24
3–1   Price Models   35
3–2   Possible Gold Scenarios for One Year: $(500)^{250}$ 38
3–3   Key Components of Price Changes   41
3–4   Model Test Design: Reducing/Specifying Price Scenarios   44
4–1   Some Types of Price Scenarios   51
4–2   The Price Model Schools   57
4–3   The Ramdom Walk Price Model   60
4–4   The Sequential Walk Model   63
4–5   The Price Vector Price Model   65
4–6   Simple Price Vector Model—Data Collection   67
4–7   Simple Price Vector Model—Data Generation   69
5–1   The Complete Trading System   147
5–2   The Monies Management System   149
5–3   The Selection Management System   153
5–4   The Research and Development System   155
5–5   The Portfolio Administration System   157

LIST OF TABLES

1–1   Examples of Timing Methods   10

1–2   Sample Operational Trading Program   13

2–1   Portfolio Simulation for Stock Trades   28

2–2   Trade Simulation Summaries for Multiple Parameter Values   31

4–1   Random Walk Model, Price Change Values; 20 Cells (Values)   72

4–2   Random Walk Model, Price Change Values; 50 Cells (Values)   75

4–3   Sequential Walk Model, Price Change Values; 50 Cells (Values)   76

4–4   Simple Price Vector Model, Vector/Cell Information; Vector-Run Random Walk Price Distributions   78

4–5   Random Walk Model, Price Change Values; 50 Cells (Values)   83

4–6   Sequential Walk Model, Price Change Values; 50 Cells (Values)   86

4–7   Simple Price Vector Model, Vector/Cell Information; Vector-Run Random Walk Price Distributions   87

4–8   Random Walk Model, Price Change Values; 50 Cells (Values)   95

4–9   Generated Prices for Apple Computer (AAPL) from Actual Sideways Market   106

4–10   Random Walk Model, Price Change Values; 40 Cells (Values)   114

4–11   Generated Prices for Apple Computer (AAPL) from Actual Uptrend Market   115

4–12   Random Walk Model, Price Change Values; 60 Cells (Values), Apple Computer   120

4–13   Random Walk Model, Price Change Values; 60 Cells (Values), Reebok International   127

4–14   Sequential Walk Model, Price Change Values; 60 Cells (Values)   132

4–15   Simple Price Vector Model, Vector/Cell Information; Vector-Run Random Walk Price Distributions   137

LIST OF CHARTS

4–1   Downtrend Prices—Low Volatility   52

4–2   Sideways Prices—High Volatility   53

4–3   Uptrend Prices—High Volatility   54

4–4   Downtrend—Low Volatility (1994)   55

4–5   Japenese Yen—Continuous Contract (01/01/95–10/06/95)   71

4–6   Random Walk Model—(Open–Low)/(High–Low) Japanese Yen—
        Continuous Contract (01/01/95–10/06/95)   73

4–7   Random Walk Model—Three Series—Japanese Yen—Continuous
        Contract (01/01/95–10/06/95)   74

4–8   Amdahl Corp. (AMH), 1990 Prices   82

4–9   Amdahl Corp. (AMH), 1990 Random Walk Model—
        (Open–Low)/(High–Low)   84

4–10   Amdahl Corp. (AMH), 1990 Random Walk Model—Three Series   85

4–11   Apple Computer (1992) Daily Prices in Sideways Market   92

4–12   Apple Computer (October 1990–April 1991) Daily Prices
        in Uptrend   93

4–13   Apple Computer (January 1993–October 1993) Daily Prices
        in Downtrend   94

4–14   Random Walk Model—Generated Prices for Apple Computer (AAPL)
        from Actual Sideways Markets (Example #1)   96

4–15   Random Walk Model—Generated Prices for Apple Computer (AAPL)
        from Actual Sideways Markets (Example #2)   97

4–16   Random Walk Model—Generated Prices for Apple Computer (AAPL)
        from Actual Sideways Markets (Example #3)   98

4–17   Random Walk Model—Generated Prices for Apple Computer (AAPL)
        from Actual Sideways Markets (Example #4)   99

4–18   Random Walk Model—Generated Prices for Apple Computer (AAPL)
        from Actual Sideways Markets (Example #5)   100

4–19   Random Walk Model—Generated Prices for Apple Computer (AAPL)
        from Actual Sideways Markets (Example #6)   101

4–20   Random Walk Model—Generated Prices for Apple Computer (AAPL)
        from Actual Sideways Markets (Example #7)   102

4–21   Random Walk Model—Generated Prices for Apple Computer (AAPL)
        from Actual Sideways Markets (Example #8)   103

4–22   Random Walk Model—Generated Prices for Apple Computer (AAPL) from Actual Sideways Markets (Example #9)   104

4–23   Random Walk Model—Generated Prices for Apple Computer (AAPL) from Actual Sideways Markets (Example #10)   105

4–24   Random Walk Model—Generated Prices for Apple Computer (AAPL) from Actual Uptrend Markets (Example #1)   112

4–25   Random Walk Model—Generated Prices for Apple Computer (AAPL) from Actual Uptrend Markets (Example #2)   113

4–26   Random Walk Model—Generated Prices for Apple Computer (AAPL) from Actual Downtrend Markets (Example #1)   122

4–27   Random Walk Model—Generated Prices for Apple Computer (AAPL) from Actual Downtrend Markets (Example #2)   123

4–28   Reebok International, Ltd (RBK), 1994–95 Prices   126

4–29   Random Walk Model—Generated Prices for Reebok International (RBK) from Actual Uptrend Prices (Example #1)   129

4–30   Random Walk Model—Generated Prices for Reebok International (RBK) from Actual Uptrend Prices (Example #2)   130

4–31   Random Walk Model—Generated Prices for Reebok International (RBK) from Actual Uptrend Prices (Example #3)   131

4–32   Sequential Walk Model—Generated Prices for Reebok International (RBK) from Actual Uptrend Prices (Example #1)   134

4–33   Sequential Walk Model—Generated Prices for Reebok International (RBK) from Actual Uptrend Prices (Example #2)   135

4–34   Sequential Walk Model—Generated Prices for Reebok International (RBK) from Actual Uptrend Prices (Example #3)   136

4–35   Price Vector Model—Generated Prices for Reebok International (RBK) from Actual Uptrend Prices (Example #1)   141

4–36   Price Vector Model—Generated Prices for Reebok International (RBK) from Actual Uptrend Prices (Example #2)   142

4–37   Price Vector Model—Generated Prices for Reebok International (RBK) from Actual Uptrend Prices (Example #3)   143

TRADING SYSTEM ANALYSIS

Using Trading Simulations
and Generated Data to Test,
Evaluate and Predict Trading
System Performance

CHAPTER 1

Systematic Trading

All of us are systematic. Creatures of habit, we go through life performing much the same routines in many activities, social and economic: the same route to work, the same simple daily eating schedules, even the same exercise programs. Often we do these same routines to escape reformulating our plans each time, to concentrate on the activities themselves.

Similarly, for trading we desire to set up a plan that works, then implement it without further thought or tinkering. We all recognize the importance of daily execution of a trading plan, but often many of us pay short shrift to the plan itself. A poor plan, no matter how well executed, will not bring about satisfactory trading results.

This chapter will be concerned with the basic elements of a good plan for trading/investing in any auction market. Elements of the plan include risk considerations, selection of trading vehicles/candidates, return maximization, and portfolio planning and implementation. Chapter 5 will pull together concepts and system testing ideas for a complete portfolio approach.

RISK MANAGEMENT

The subject of risk is vast indeed, with many aspects and in-depth details. It ranges from individual risk preferences and attitudes toward losing money to mathematical ways of reducing aggregate portfolio losses. Here we will discuss two aspects important to traders: individual risk outlook and ways to assess risk in a portfolio. Control of risk will be addressed in the discussion on portfolio management.

Personal Risk Attitude

Trading risk is not a monolithic concept: Every trader has his or her level of risk tolerance. Some will calmly bear losses of 50 percent, others will cringe at 5 percent deductions from their accounts. The differences and reasons for this varied risk tolerance are legion: different ages, sexes, economic statuses, and even geography. But personality is probably the single most important contributor or factor in the equation. An aggressive trader—young or old, male or female—will be more willing to accept bigger losses than a conservative, introspective, retreating sort of person.

This means, whichever end of the spectrum he belongs to, the trader must acknowledge, accept, and plan for that level of risk appropriate to him. A speculative sort might plan a portfolio by diversifying over 10 items with just a little reserve capital, while a very conservative type may need to spread his investments over 100 instruments and keep a majority of his monies in cash reserve. The mechanics of this process will be discussed in the portfolio section.

Measuring/Evaluating Risk: Some Indicators

One may recognize and set his or her own risk tolerance in the portfolio (more later on how to do this), but how does the trader measure/evaluate risk in the portfolio? Once he implements risk plans, the trader must be able to measure their effectiveness.

The following is a discussion of several ways of measuring/evaluating risk in a portfolio.

Probably the best known and most used measure is the Sharpe ratio. Developed by Nobel laureate William Sharpe over 30 years ago, it is a measure of return received relative to risk encountered in the portfolio:

$$SR = \text{Average return / average risk} \quad \text{(Sharpe ratio)}$$

$$= \overline{R} \Big/ \sqrt{\sum_{1}^{N} (r_i - \overline{R})^2 \big/ (N-1)}$$

where

$$\overline{R} = \sum_{1}^{N} r_i / N$$

r_i = Return (profit) for period i.

The denominator is simply the standard deviation of returns over the N periods (years, months, over whatever basic period of time the trader examines his portfolio). Often a portfolio manager will subtract the risk-free rate of return (a common example is the current CD rate) from the return portion (numerator) of the equation, to get the risk-free adjusted (more true) return/risk ratio, indicating how much better the trader performed over putting the money in a nice safe bank.

On the good side this index rewards those results that show higher returns and/or lower risk. It also measures directly how many dollars are risked for each dollar made. However, it penalizes for growth/return above the average—the ratio considers that a deviation and adds it to the denominator, making the ratio smaller, instead of rewarding the trader and increasing the ratio for exceptional performance. Also, if the trader were to put his funds in a very meager return investment (say 6–7 percent, or just above the CD rate) that had virtually no risk, the Sharpe ratio would be unusually large, almost infinite, by unfairly emphasizing little variation in growth and making the denominator very small and the subsequent ratio very large.

Some possible alternatives to the standard deviation in the denominator: the range (high minus low) of returns over the entire period covered or the largest single losing period (magnitude only). These would help correct for penalizing normal, good but variable growth; but extremely low losses relative to low returns would be still given better Sharpe ratios than just plain low or moderate losses with large returns. The denominator is still a problem: Minimizing risk is still too large an influence over maximizing return. (A CD investment would have the highest ratio, even over a lusty growth performance with much upward growth variation but no losing periods!)

Some other indices that deemphasize profit penalization have recently come into favor.

The Calmar ratio (Terry Young) is defined as the average rate of return over the past 36 months divided by the maximum drawdown over the same period (see later discussion of drawdown), calculated monthly. It retains the benefits of the Sharpe ratio and improves it by using maximum drawdown instead of standard deviation of return (like the use of maximum losing period in the Sharpe ratio referred to above), but also suffers from a single drawdown inordinately dominating the return side of the equation.

The Sterling ratio (Deane Jones) is a variation of the Calmar ratio and is defined as the 3-year rate of return divided by −1 times the 3-year average drawdown plus 10. It offers the advantages of the Calmar ratio but also is prone to the same weaknesses as well as being calculated too infrequently.

The geographic mean has been explored by Ralph Vince and combines many of the advantages of the other indices with few of the pitfalls. Formally, the

$$\text{Geometric mean return} = \prod_{1}^{N}(1+r_i)$$

$$= (1+r_1)*(1+r_2)*(1+r_3)*\cdots*(1+r_N)$$

where

r_i = rate of return (expressed in fraction, not percent) for period i (e.g., −.10 = loss of 10 percent; +.16 = gain of 16 percent)

The mean shows the result on the portfolio of an initial investment and the end result: 1.0 growing to 5.0 means a 400 percent increase in the account, after losses. The trader must convert, if necessary, monthly gains to increases/decreases from the period begin point, not the very initial period value. Traders not reinvesting profits each period could be penalized with this mean.

One criticism that applies both to the Sharpe ratio and the geometric mean is the idea of orderedness: an alternating mixture of gains and losses may give the same ratio and mean as one that had all gaining periods in a row followed by losing periods in a row, but to the trader in the real world the latter group of loss strings would be unsatisfactory and less valuable than a mildly mixed group of gains and losses. For example, if we have two systems with monthly percentage returns with (even nearly) the same cumulative returns results, with

System A returns of: +12, −6, +12, −6   and

System B returns of: +12, +12, −6, −6,

System A's would be far more desirable, as two losses of 6 percent in a row make it more likely for larger *cumulative* losing periods to occur for System B than for System A.

This last example led the author (back in 1967) to devise a measure of risk that related to the trader's true worry: Cumulative losses, at the beginning or at any subsequent point of trading, might mount to such a large size that the trader or his customers would lose faith in the trading system (fearing a total tap-out or loss loomed in the near future), and thus the trader would halt trading. The drawdown statistic, a measure of cumulative loss from any intermediate point (usually a peak to trough measure), can be used by the trader to monitor when performance is on track or getting worse than expected. Note that the statistic is tracked on the same time basis the trader uses (e.g., daily) and is not a periodic measure, (e.g., return per month/quarter); rather it is measured over time periods and is concerned only with magnitude.

It turns out that drops/reactions/drawdowns from intermediate peaks (see examples 1, 2, 3, 4, and 5 in Figure 1–1) can be measured easily (just peak to trough, the trough being the minimal point before the next new peak) and accurately describe, with a little math-statistics (the drawdowns are exponentially distributed), what to expect in the future for the portfolio. The following little table is an approximate but handy guide for what to expect about drawdowns when they do occur:

Size of Drawdown (%)	Probability of Occurrence (%)
X	50
$2.3X$	10
$3.0X$	5
$4.3X$	1

where

X = Average drawdown

For example, if the trader found from past history that the average drawdown was 10 percent, then when drawdowns occured he would expect them to be 10 percent or larger 50 percent of the time. A drop of 2.3*10 percent = 23 percent (or larger) would occur only 10 percent of the time , and one of 3.0*10 = 30 percent would happen only 5 percent of the time.

The advantage of this statistic is that it measures risk only, so a trader can focus on risk containment solely with this statistic. One negative is that it is measured only when reactions/drawdowns actually occur, and so decisions cannot be made by rote each month, for example. Also, it does not incorporate return as a complete portfolio measure.

FIGURE 1-1

Measuring Risk: Drawdowns in a Portfolio

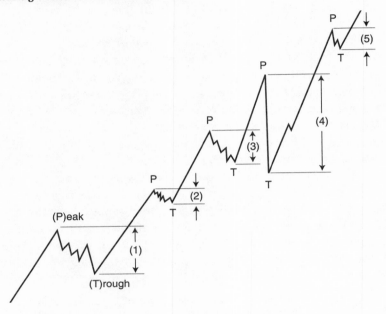

A New Return/Risk Index

The main disadvantage of the Sharpe ratio is that its denominator has too much influence, and division can create warped or weird numbers. The drawdown statistic needs to incorporate returns, not just concentrate on risk. Neither allows for customization, emphasis, or personalization of return or risk for each trader.

The following index, the Gain/Pain Index, may solve the problems of both. Formally,

$$GPI = \left(\lambda * Gains + (1 - \lambda) * losses\right) / \left(|Gains| + |Losses|\right) * 100$$

where

    Gains are positive and are total or gross gains

    Losses are negative and are total or gross losses

    |Losses| = Magnitude (absolute value) of losses; of course, gains are already positive

and

> λ = Weight (emphasis) on *return* selected by the trader's as the desired factor, and can vary from 0 to 1.0
>
> 1 – λ = Weight on *risk* as the desired factor

It is simply return minus risk, with a weight λ (importance set by the trader) on returns or gains to personalize or customize for each trader. The higher he places the value on risk, 1 – λ, the more losses dominate the equation and turn the index toward negative values.

For instance, if the trader were very speculative, totally emphasizing return, he would let λ = 1.0 and totally ignore risk in the numerator, but be cognizant that more (net) gains over losses would still improve his index. A system having all gains, no losses, and λ =1.0 would have a GPI of 100. In the other extreme, a totally risk-conscious trader would set λ = 0 and ignore gains, to the point where the index could only be negative or zero (no losses). Obviously he would opt for trading systems that netted near-zero losses. Both extremes are ignoring either risk or return, to the trader's possible detriment (his choice, though).

Most traders would place themselves in between the two extremes, with a slant toward either return (λ) or risk (1 – λ) orientation. For example, if the trader gave equal weight to gains and losses, he would let λ = 0.5, and, obviously, the more gains came above losses the better (and greater plus value) for the index.

One variation of the above formula is to drop the 100 multiplier (it is just a constant factor anyway to scale the index from –100 to +100) and remove the denominator, with emphasis on the relative importance or personalization of risk and return to the trader.

SELECTION OF TRADING CANDIDATES

A second, very important element of the systematic approach to investing is the selection of candidates for inclusion in the portfolio.

The first question that pops up is what markets to deal in, and how much (dollars) to place in each. Figure 1–2 displays an "investment speedometer." When the trader moves his investment "car" at 0–10, he is dealing with low risk but also low return vehicles, such as government instruments/bonds, municipal bonds, corporate bonds and the like. In the other extreme, the returns are high, but so too are the loss potentials.

FIGURE 1-2

Investment Speedometer

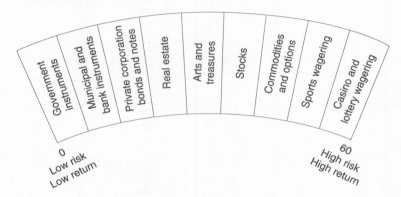

Commodities (because of low margin or deposit requirements), options, and wagering well embody this high-speed area.

Not only are there varying amounts of risk and reward in each area, but they change over time. It is a moot point whether these changes are predictable and how long they last: Real estate was once thought to be a high-return (leveraged) area with little downside risk. Many homeowners in the 1980s and 1990s found out otherwise, as the value of their homes at best stayed unchanged but often dropped dramatically. Likewise, seemingly stable muni bonds and other bank-backed instruments have gone south in a big way. And the opposite has occurred: real doldrum areas—like the stock market in the 70s, bouncing between 500 and 1000 on the Dow Industrials—have turned into soaring eagles in the 80s and 90s. Commodities, on the other hand, have had very sporadic performances: spectacular trended years, followed by the doldrums, then good years again.

Thus there is the question of which markets to invest in. A "switching device" is needed, some sort of index that alerts the trader to relative return-and-risk potential in each market at any point in time.

The cardinal rule of asset allocation is that, since no one really knows which investment will pay off big, diversification is always called for.

The first step then, is to determine how much to allocate to each market. Relative risks and returns of each will weigh in the decision, much as the trader views the return/risk measures for each instrument. (Asset allocation will be addressed later). If the trader will be dealing with only one market, such as commodities or stocks, this (market allocation) question does not arise.

Once the market allocation and switching problem has been dealt with, the question of selecting individual instruments arises. Again, does the trader choose stocks with the largest return history or potential; stocks with the lowest risk; as many stocks as his portfolio can handle; or high-priced or low-priced stocks?

In terms of candidate selection, experience has shown that individual investment candidates with the following checklist provide the investment pot with the best stew:

1. *Large relative cumulative price moves.* This is an especially positive feature for trend-following timing methods, but also for aggressive contrary techniques.

2. *Low/suitable price volatility.* The less prices sharply diverge, the better timing methods can track and optimize entry points.

3. *Good liquidity.* The trader needs to enter and exit without getting significantly adverse price moves because his volume is a large part of total trading volume.

4. *Include many instruments.* In keeping with asset-allocation and risk-reduction principles, as many numbers of instruments should be included as fit other criteria (e.g., have a certain minimum cumulative trend history, for return maximization).

5. *Include many types of instruments.* The trader should diversify over as many different *types* of markets, to maximize return opportunities and also reduce risk.

TIMING METHODS

No other aspect of investing commands the attention or ardor of traders more than the timing of buys and sells. They might have enough capital to trade, have properly allocated monies to many investments and kept good reserves, and may unswervingly follow all signals, but if the *timing* of trades is off, they may actually even lose.

There are many methods for timing trades: Some are designed for certain types of markets; others reflect the trader's personality and habits. Generally speaking there are four schools or types of timing methods meant for different markets.

Some like to *forecast* prices and conditions as accurately as possible, then take positions favorable to the projected price level. Fundamentalists use supply-demand data (such as carry over stock, government reports, monthly crop reports, weather projections, etc.), while technical analysts use prices and price formations to project prices.

Trend followers tend to look for long-term price movements, and their methods range from simple chart line projections to mathematical formulas such as moving averages and other statistical forecasting tools.

No-trend or random market afficionados are users of the *contrary* timing method; they believe that prices do not significantly trend much of the time and so look for price aberrations (far removed from the present predominant price level) to take advantage of, hoping prices will recover to the current major price area.

A fourth school, *pattern detection,* looks for more complex price events, everything from wavelike motion to long-developing shapes on charts (heads and shoulders, for example).

Examples of each each of the four timing-method schools discussed above can be found in Table 1–1.

TABLE 1–1

Examples of Timing Methods

Name	Type	Position Taking Formula	Profit Mode
Adaptive forecast	Forecast	Forecast of large price jumps/drops	Projected price
Fundamental	Forecast	Supply/demand price projection versus current price	Projected price
Box size breakout	Trend	Prices outside period range	Opposite condition
Moving average	Trend	Prices over/under moving average	Opposite condition
Contrary bands	Contrary	Prices way over/under moving average	Current major price level or opposite condition
Relative strength	Contrary	Index too high or too low	Index midvalue(50) or opposite condition
Chart formations	Pattern	Familiar/significant shape	Projected condition
Elliot wave	Pattern	Minimum up/down waves	Projected waves

PORTFOLIO MANAGEMENT

The three elements above (risk, selection, and trade timing) constitute the main components of a trading system. The trader needs an overall plan to put these elements into profitable use. The plan involves managing monies, incorporating trading decisions, and implementing administrative/bookkeeping matters.

Initial and Reinvestment Monies

The first steps are administrative in nature. The trader must first put together enough cash to fund investments in enough instruments and carry sufficient reserves for losses and possibly margin needs. The minimum cash amount required to start the portfolio is usually arrived at by first determining the funds necessary to support N separate, and hopefully independent, investments. The largest single requirement is first calculated (say, $10,000 cash/margin is needed for a Standard and Poor's (S&P) futures contract; or $30 per stock average price level times 100 shares, or $3,000). Next, the number of separate investments (N) is set (usually a minimum of 10; often no more than 50—statistics tell us that those numbers are the minimum and maximum to get good diversification, with fewer than 10 resulting in erratic returns, and more than 50 having little improvement on risk reduction). Then the cash investment needs are calculated as the product of the largest single investment times the number of investments. The cash reserve is usually set at some multiple of the cash investment, at least 1:1, preferably 2:1, and as high as 5–10:1 for very conservative accounts. For the above S&P example—for a large individual instrument investment of $10,000, 10 investments, and 50 percent cash reserve—the total portfolio cash requirement would be 10*$10,000+ 1*$100,000= $200,000 total capital needed.

The reasons behind the account cash setup are thus: there will be at least 10 investments of equal size with at least 50 percent cash in reserve, to get the benefits of diversification (10 investments); unbiased growth (equal dollar size investment positions) to maximize growth *and* reduce risk; and reserve power (50 percent in reserve) to guard against losing periods, which will happen (but we don't know when).

Profits should be reinvested at no less than 10 percent increases in account value, and no more than 100 percent, to guard against too much accounting and error potential and imperceptible improvement in the account (the lower, 10 percent figure), and not taking advantage of compounding at the higher end (the 100 percent number).

It has also been found prudent to reinvest profits equally amongst the competing investments, again to obtain maximum growth and minimum risk at the same time (often, both do not occur together!).

Other Administrative Steps

An account must be opened with a brokerage to transact the trades. It is recommended to sign up with a good quality discount house (in business a long time, good in executions, well capitalized, quickly responsive to trader requests, has low fees, and has information available on all aspects of investments if possible) or a large brokerage where the broker is especially attentive or has extras that are desirable (good trading methods, quick news retrieval, good services in general). Certain account forms must be filled in, telephone numbers established/obtained, and other like and sundry matters.

Running the Daily Operation

Before running the portfolio in real time the trader must run his timing program historically up until the current day to find out the latest variables' values, to put into an operational/real-time timing program. For example, if he used a moving average program, he must have the latest price averages to work with at the current point in time, and to obtain these averages he must run the program from far enough in the past through to the present time.

Also, from time to time the trader may add or subtract new monies and new instruments or delete/modify current ones (such as futures or options contracts that expire and must be replaced) in the portfolio.

He must design his operational program to provide him with buy-sell information quickly and accurately for each new day. Table 1–2 displays a typical operational trading program. The method is named on top, with perhaps some description to differentiate/highlight its use underneath. Investment positions it can take (here longs as well as shorts) are noted next. Finally, the captions conclude with the date to which the advice applies.

TABLE 1-2

Sample Operational Trading Program

GOAL: MAXIMIZE RETURN W/ACCEPTABLE RISK

LONGS AND SHORTS

ACTIONS FOR CLOSE ON TRADE DAY AFTER
960909

DAY NO. 61

SYM	CURR POS	DATE IN	PRICE IN	CURRENT PRICE	FORECAST CL. PRICE	NEW BUY STP CL. PRICE	NEW SELL STP CL. PRICE	CURR POS PROFIT	NEW ACTION
---	----	------	----------	---------	-----------	----------	----------	--------	-----
ABRX	+1	960802	56.87500	53.25000	52.99596	0.00000	47.02268	-3.62500	0
ALR	-1	960628	18.25000	17.12500	17.19455	19.11134	0.00000	+1.12500	0
APOL	-1	960402	25.33300	23.25000	23.09638	26.59885	0.00000	+2.08300	0
ASPT	+1	960802	54.00000	52.00000	52.06358	0.00000	45.28378	-2.00000	0
ASTF	-1	960625	23.37500	23.75000	23.76942	26.70728	0.00000	-0.37500	0
CAMP	+1	960826	10.12500	11.25000	11.23660	0.00000	9.85231	+1.12500	0
CCE	+0	0	0.00000	39.25000	39.26287	44.18782	34.25210	+0.00000	0
CMRE	+1	940616	3.68800	11.00000	11.04150	0.00000	9.52211	+7.31200	0
CSCC	+1	960802	69.87500	68.12500	68.26961	0.00000	59.20115	-1.75000	0
CSN	+1	960326	42.87500	48.25000	48.59011	0.00000	41.44526	+5.37500	0
CTYS	-1	960402	19.00000	27.00000	26.63816	31.37123	0.00000	+11.83300	0
CXC	+1	960802	35.00000	30.50000	30.17111	0.00000	27.30687	-4.50000	0
DL2	-1	960402	39.58300	27.75000	27.75146	31.26117	0.00000	+11.83300	0
DGPC	+1	960223	20.00000	48.00000	47.91346	0.00000	42.09636	+28.00000	0
EAGL	+1	950515	7.37500	23.25000	23.56074	0.00000	19.67178	+15.87500	0
EGOI	+1	960805	17.50000	16.62500	16.83339	0.00000	14.09451	-0.87500	0
GAL	-1	960716	22.37500	28.25000	28.69245	30.66780	0.00000	-5.87500	0
HBOC	-1	960402	50.12500	54.75000	55.15316	60.62513	0.00000	-4.62500	0
HFS	+1	950712	21.00000	58.75000	58.78933	0.00000	51.22820	+37.75000	0
HRC	+0	0	0.00000	35.00000	35.42952	38.30417	29.69140	+0.00000	0
HSY	+0	0	0.00000	88.25000	88.64542	98.38881	76.26588	+0.00000	0
IMPX	1	960723	5.87500	4.81300	4.75509	5.57488	0.00000	+1.06200	0
JMED	+1	960726	31.25000	42.50000	43.04496	0.00000	36.00616	+11.25000	0
JNJ	-1	960402	47.62500	49.87500	50.00419	55.85287	0.00000	-2.25000	0
KNT	-1	960711	17.00000	17.37500	16.47013	21.95464	0.00000	-0.37500	0
LIZ	-1	941220	17.62500	34.25000	34.23975	38.61529	0.00000	-16.62500	0
LOHO	-1	960723	16.75000	17.25000	17.51807	18.73026	0.00000	-0.50000	0
MCAF	+1	960606	44.75000	61.00000	60.81444	0.00000	53.65147	+16.25000	0
MIR	+0	0	0.00000	23.75000	23.80636	26.61017	20.62682	+0.00000	0
MONE	+1	951114	17.90000	23.31300	23.24131	0.00000	20.50612	+5.41300	0
NATR	+1	950804	15.16700	20.37500	19.72232	0.00000	19.12419	+5.20800	0
NAUT	+1	960628	28.75000	25.75000	25.46422	0.00000	23.07068	-3.00000	0
NEC	-1	960625	13.87500	18.62500	18.84203	20.41361	0.00000	-4.75000	0
NKE	+0	0	0.00000	113.25000	114.61953	123.99467	96.11421	+0.00000	0
PAIR	+1	960802	65.75000	68.25000	68.69077	0.00000	58.70679	+2.50000	0
PCOL	+1	960812	20.75000	19.00000	18.87465	0.00000	16.84877	-1.75000	0
PFE	+0	0	0.00000	73.37500	73.84133	81.44323	63.13055	+0.00000	0
RB	+1	940617	7.12500	25.25000	25.44307	0.00000	21.65822	+18.12500	0
RIG	+0	0	0.00000	55.37500	55.40980	62.29767	48.28991	+0.00000	0
RXL	+1	951103	12.75000	14.00000	14.00761	0.00000	12.21116	+1.25000	0
SLM	+0	0	0.00000	73.00000	72.89189	82.53088	63.97364	+0.00000	0
TGET	+1	960828	35.25000	31.75000	31.67219	0.00000	27.88689	-3.50000	0
THI	+0	0	0.00000	38.25000	38.40843	42.67849	33.08215	+0.00000	0
TIF	+1	960514	37.25000	37.62500	38.38910	0.00000	31.30210	+0.37500	0

13

The rows list each investment vehicle (here stocks) followed, and the columns dictate information and advice about these instruments.

Certain basic information is required. The current position for each instrument, the date and price of entry, and the current price are all needed for administrative checking and analyses of current results.

Some additional information about the "state" of the instrument is sometimes added in the middle columns. Here I have inserted a column titled "forecast (of next) close price" in the middle of the table. This lets the trader know where prices are headed and how strong they are.

Most important, though, are the "action" columns (here identified as "New buy stop close price", and "New sell stop close price"), which are intended to tell the trader where to buy and sell that day. In this example, ABRX is currently long so a short position would be taken at the close if it closed there at 47.02268 (rounded down to 47 even when placing or considering an actual order) or lower. Similarly, ALB is currently short, and would be bought at 19.11134 (19-1/8 , the closest tradeable number) or higher on the close.

Finally, current position profits and a "new action" column may be added , to inform the trader of trades that were triggered on the prior day's close, in case he missed those signals called for the prior day. Before the day begins, he may wish to review the list and underline action prices possibly within reach that day and to circle (for extra emphasis) those positions very close to being triggered.

Discipline

To make the system work, (to make the car run), it takes command management: unswerving control, "gas" and "steady as she goes" steering, to make and keep the account profitable.

Many have said that management discipline, the unending adherence to the trading system's procedures, is 90 percent of trading success. The plan calls for proper timing of trades and efficient diversification of assets may be great, but if the trader cannot follow timing signals and correctly commit capital to trades, he might as well throw out the whole trading system.

The trader is part of and parcel to the trading system. Like a cart without a cooperative horse, the system will not go anywhere without a disciplined trader. Traders do not go through as epic a struggle as many heros of the past like Washington and Napoleon, but sometimes they feel powerful battles have emptied their wallet reserves! Successful ones do have one thing going for them, however: the rules give them extra strength to see another day. "Know thyself." says the ancient Greek oracle, and this is sound advice even for traders: Perceive your limitations and strengths, and follow good emotion-controlling rules of behavior.

The following list of 12 disciplines can take the trader down the path to righteous, profitable trading.

1. *Follow all timing signals.* First and foremost, the trader must follow *all* timing signals and must commit the amount of capital called for by his allocation procedures. He must not let judgment enter (too early/late an entry, no entry, several entries, etc.) lest the one big gain be omitted or severely cut short.

2. *Continue to trade even with losing streaks.* A reemphasis of item 1., a trader must not be discouraged by losing streaks (they are built into the long-term equity growth plan and are bound to occur over and over again). Every timing system has periods of whipsaw losses. Trend-following methods like moving averages get tangled up in tight trading ranges and seemingly unending losses, whereas contrary methods experience either huge losses or strings of moderate-to-small losses in long, trended markets.

3. *Do not change methods whimsically, yet keep an open mind.* The trader should not change methods—timing, allocation, or risk control—due to short-term results. Even though he may feel the trades are not working out in the short term, the long-term results account for short-term ups and downs. On the other hand, if a long-term study has shown a new timing method to be really significantly superior to the current one, the trader may wish to replace the latter.

4. *Shut out outside influences.* Boardroom tips, news events, other traders' plans, or personal problems must not be allowed to interfere with the execution of trading system procedures.

5. *Treat trading as a game.* The trader must consider gains and losses to be just numbers in a great Monopoly® game. The correct strategy (the winning trading system) will lead him to own Park Place and Boardwalk.

6. *Relieve pressures.* He must have the ability to relieve the pressures of trading life by crying, laughing and generally downplaying the importance of trading results.

7. *Have confidence.* The trader must develop and exude confidence. Psychology works in trading as it does in tennis: The more he believes that he'll win, the more probable it is (if nothing else, because he holds on throughout the system's life, and his account is profitable at the end). Often tennis matches are won on a turnaround in momentum, that time in the game when the player on top starts coasting and his opponent starts building up points, games, and momentum, to eventually overtake and beat the leader.

  The market may at times turn in many different, unexpected and unpleasant ways, but if the trader holds on through bad times, he will be rewarded with good times to follow.

8. *Act promptly.* The trader should always promptly and decisively execute trades. He should not procrastinate or waver in placing orders, lest loss of time alone give him poor execution prices, and less profit or losses.

9. *Drive avarice and fear out.* He should not be greedy, and 'ad lib' his trades and hold out for more profits, for such actions always lead to less profits or even losses. Similarly, the trader should toss out excessive fear (normal fear, a moderate dose, is all right; it promotes humility—see 12th point). Being too fearful or timid could end up costing him a good gain, often occuring when times look most bleak.

10. *Become unemotional.* If possible, the best course a trader can steer is to be totally unemotional about every trade and every trading day. If he is patient and unswerving in his commitment to follow each signal and rule, his reward will be good long-term profits.

11. *Show humility.* The trader should have humility. Just because he is on the investment scene, the market is not going to rush to him and give him profits. He will have to fight, get scars, and earn his way to good long-term profits.

12. *Reject approval and disapproval.* The trader does not need, and should avoid, the approval or admiration of others. If he succumbs to general boardroom approval, or even analysis of his trades, he will be doomed to losses. Admiration and swooning over his results by others can have the adverse effect of making him vulnerable to taking his own personal advice, delaying execution of trades, holding onto gains and losses too long, and rendering him unprepared and unable to handle losing periods later on. Conversely, if the trader shrinks away from and cannot execute his own system's signals when others show disbelief, disapproval, or jealousy, many good trades may be lost.

IN SUMMARY

A systematic approach to trading was outlined in this chapter. Key components included risk attitudes, assessment, capital allocation, and control; selection of investments; timing programs; and portfolio management. A whole portfolio plan brings together these components into a workable and winning trading program. This plan was detailed, from initial and reinvestment monies allocation procedures, to administrative procedures and daily operational control. A list of discipline habits was presented to help the trader run the program smoothly and accurately.

However, we did not address the central problem of how to optimize the overall performance of the portfolio (except with regard to risk diversification), nor even to find out what to accurately expect for investment performance. These two most important aspects are addressed in the coming chapters. It turns out the trader must test his timing methods and subsequent portfolio values on a set of price scenarios that realistically, accurately, and fully reflect the *future,* not the past. With great numbers of reasonable scenarios he can then accurately determine which timing methods and settings will give him the most profits.

CHAPTER 2

Actual versus Simulated Trading Results

The importance of having a (many) good timing method(s) cannot be overemphasized. In plain language, if the trader cannot time his buys and sells well, he will get unsatisfactory profits.

It is not enough to simply pick a method and use any parameter settings: Every method has "control knobs" or parameters/variables that make the method respond well or poorly to the stock or commodity being analyzed. It is up to the trader to properly set those knobs so he will know when to buy and sell accurately.

However, it is well known that price movements change and that using a method with the same parameter settings will yield changing trade results that flip-flop between good and bad (rarely all good, sometimes all bad).

Most frustrating to traders is the situation in which they test their timing methods on prior (historical) price data, then apply the method to the current time, only to obtain bad trading results. Or worse (and this does happen often), good real-time, actual market trading results will be followed by poor trading results.

This is the paradox facing every systems (and nonsystems, such as fundamentalist) trader: How can he assure himself of good real-time trading results in the future? If it is not possible to always to have goodly profits each period, could he assure himself of at least consistent (even if modest) profits or great trading periods with very small (relatively speaking) losses in others? Perhaps it is too much to expect profits galore, unending streaks of profits monotonously climbing upward (see more realistic expectations, next chapter). Then again, he is in the market to make money, and if there are not good and consistent profit opportunities, maybe he should look elsewhere.

We shall explore the world of trading simulations by examining their intent, how traders use them in research and fare in actual trading, and how they are used in other businesses.

GOOD SIMULATIONS, BAD RESULTS

The basic procedure for a trader using simulations is to take a trading method and test various combinations of its variables/parameters on historical data, find the best winning setting, and then use that method with the good setting in real time. He is assuming that the setting that was successful in the past will continue to be so in the future.

What happens most of the time? Figure 2–1 shows two periods, a historical period (A) and a real-time period (B), when the trader actually traded the method. The historical one could be characterized by very smooth-acting, long-term trends. His moving average method did well with almost every setting, especially with medium-term averages that caught the big moves early and kept most of the profits. So he opts to use a medium-term average in the present period, with real funds at stake.

What happens? The markets suddenly turn choppy, and his moving average method quickly changes trading positions for him in following these rapid market changes. But the little trends do not last long, and he finds he has continually entered relatively late (bought high and sold low), only to see the short-lasting trend turn abruptly the other way. He ends up with many small-to-moderate losses, unlike the few-but-large trend profits he would have made in the historical or test period.

What went wrong? In hindsight, his method in the historical period caught the new price moves sometime after they had bottomed or topped out, but the new moves went far, so he ended up getting much of the new move and consistent profit after consistent profit. But the moves in the new period did not last long, and thus he ended up buying near the end of upmoves and selling near the bottom of downmoves. The schematic at the bottom of the figure tells us the whole story: On average in the current, real-time period, the trader was selling low, near the bottom of a typical

FIGURE 2-1

Historical Tests and Real-Time Trading with the Moving Average Method

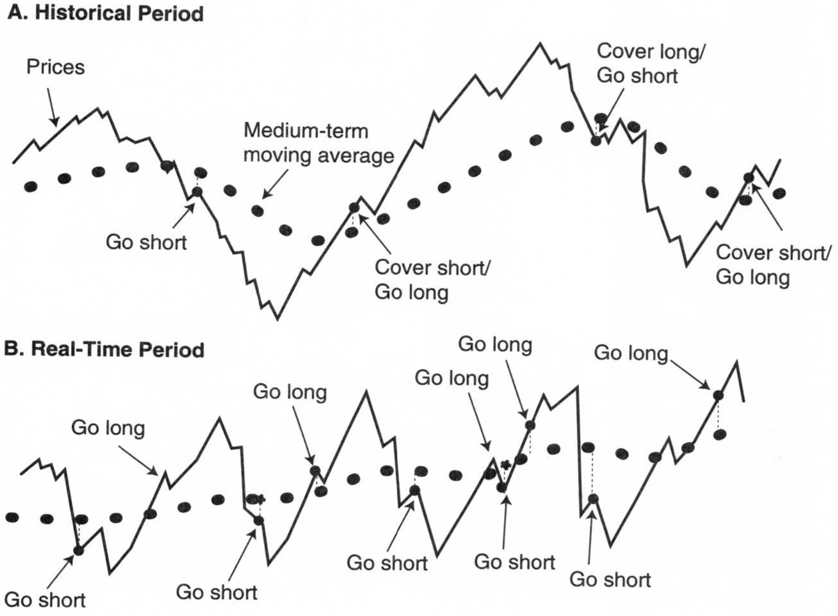

A. Historical Period

B. Real-Time Period

downtrend, and reversing to a long position at a high(er) price—in effect selling low and buying high, a steadily losing proposition.

REAL TRADERS IN LIVE TIMES

How have traders fared in actual trading?

In commodities, individual speculators have been at the game for many years. Overall, according to many sources, only 10–20 percent have shown net profits for their accounts. That means that, for the other 80–90 percent, either costs have been high and/or their trading approaches have not worked.

In the brokerages, and for the general customer accounts I have had that trade by their own devices, the figures hold pretty much to the 10–20 percent net gains figure. Of the few who use systematic methods, perhaps they have shown an improvement to 30–40 percent net profitable accounts. None, however, have shown consistent, strong growth over time.

In the professional ranks there are those who trade on the floor and those who are at a distance. Again, through a casual survey, in my years of personal contact and review of news and other sources, I have found only a handful who have shown net profits, and none who have had strong profits each year. The same applies to managed account professionals. As an industry, they have experienced good and bad times, fat years and droughts.

Especially succulent profit periods occurred during 1973–75 when poor crops combined with great new demand (e.g., Russians for wheat) to propel prices upward to double, quadruple, and more trader profits. Markets moved together at many points in time, crashed in 1974, and took many speculators to the sidelines and emptied their wallets. Across the board, it was the greatest bull market, certainly in modern times. Some speculators did quite well, with a tenfold increase in their accounts in one year not uncommon.

The years 1979–81 saw a different scenario, but replete with many profit opportunities due to inflation. Interest rates skyrocketed to 18 percent, gold and silver went through the roof (gold from $100 to over $800 per ounce, while silver jetted from $5 to over $50 per ounce), the grains had a drought period, and currencies, new on the scene, provided some good trends for new traders.

Again, in 1988–91 a sprinkling of varied trends (especially in soybeans, 1988–89; a steady uptrend , doubling cattle prices; a sharp, short run up and down for crude oil; and some downtrends in gold, silver, and coffee) provided overall profit opportunities for the managed account professional.

The managed account industry did show sustained and large profits during those three periods (few managers were around, though, in 1975 to profit from that momentus time) but had few profitable outcomes in between (mostly losing years) and have experienced weak results for the past six years, 1991–96. Press releases from the managed account groups have talked about 15 percent overall returns per year, through 1991, competitive with stock market mutual funds. However, since that point in time returns have shrunk and probably show no more than 9 percent overall per year average, with many lean years in between the three big trend blips referred to previously. Without the bull years of 1973–75, overall results may even be as low as 4–5 percent, barely competitive with CDs and far more volatile!

Because fund managers have proprietary methods it is hard to say how many use systematic approaches and have tested their methods extensively. As an industry, though, they have shown no more prowess than the individual user of systems, and have ended up with mediocre net long-term trading results.

CURRENT SIMULATION USAGE

How do traders use simulations now to perfect their trading methods for real-time use?

All researchers start by testing their methods on some historical period, to generally see how their methods react and perhaps find some set of parameters that makes the system perform well for that period. Such a test was made by our intrepid moving average advocate in Figure 2–1, and he ended up settling on an intermediate (say, 20-day) moving average that worked well in that period, to use in subsequent, real-life trading.

Research styles differ from individual to individual. There are generally two camps of simulation testing, depicted in situations A and B in Figure 2–2.

Camp A believes that by testing and optimizing a method over all historical price data he will be prepared for the future: the assumption is that the future will be much like the past, and if he can tailor his method to take care of all past scenarios he will do just fine in the future. A subgroup believes in restricting the selection of past history to those periods the researcher in his best judgment believes will recur. In that way he is "improving" the quality of his method's performance, by optimizing/fitting the method to what he, the "expert", believes the future holds for price movements.

A second, more vocal camp, believes the first leaves much to be desired and adds some testing. Adherents claim the test-all-and-optimize approach is simply curve fitting/hindsight and promotes wishful trade results rather than a realistic, unbiased projection of results. They acknowledge that a system developer must develop on—and tailor his method to react to—price movements and that he needs some data to develop/set the system parameters. They thus assign part of historical data for development

F I G U R E   2–2

Simulation Testing Approaches

A. Test All/Representative History

**B. Test Representative History, Then
Walk (Test) Forward**

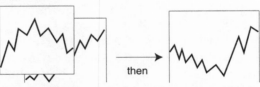

Test representative period   Test optimum historical setting
and optimize   on next period(s)

C. Test All Possible Scenarios

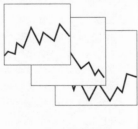 

Test historical   and   Test **MANY** future scenarios

. . . then optimize   . . . thousands/millions

but the rest or another portion must be set aside for fresh or unbiased testing, as if the trader were real-time in the market.

This second testing phase would use the best setting from the first
or developmental period, and the acid test would be how the method

performed in the second period. It would have the added benefit of a "paper" test of the trader's money without real money at stake, and he could draw the same conclusions about usefulness of the system without risking a dime.

The heart of the assumption here is statistical in nature. Statisticians like to test two groups of data then draw conclusions about the similarities between each. Here the trader would be testing whether the method and its results "hold water," that they (the results) are essentially the same from one historical period to the next. The label "walk forward" has been pinned to this approach because the trader is developing the method in one period, then moving forward in time to simulate his taking the method into the real world for an acid test (but on paper, lucky for him).

Both methods, however, have large and similar drawbacks. Camp A, test all and optimize from all historical data, basically suffers from too little data, not curve fitting as Camp B claims. If a researcher tests and optimizes over one year or five, or several different periods, these are still limited periods of time and price situations. Statistically speaking, the sample is too small—not large enough period(s) or types of situations from which to draw conclusions.

(As an aside, statisiticians generally require at least several dozen samples to characterize or affirm the true identity of a set of data. Here there is neither enough data—only several years, up to 20 relevant years maximum; nor independent data—don't trends/moves/patterns overlap or continue over more than just one year? Isn't a string of 10 years' big trend really, in effect, just one related sample of price data?)

Camp B cannot look up its nose at Camp A, either. If its claim about the out-of-sample period being the only true independent, testable data, then it suffers even more from lack of sufficient data (number of years or price scenarios). Moreover, it professes to an acid test—how the trader would do in actuality, in the second and supposedly new period. But the second period is *not* the future—it is the *past,* really and actually—and the trader is not interested ultimately in how the method would behave in the past, only *now* or in the *future.*

Both camps miss the point: A method must be tested on scenarios that adequately reflect/represent the future, not the past. If there were only one price pattern that ever occurred (controlled/set prices I suppose, like $40 fixed gold prices prior to 1974), then the trader would need only one test and that would indeed truly be accurate for all time. On the other hand, if there were one million possible price scenarios, the trader should research all of them, optimize for the whole set of one million, and be prepared for any one; then he would know what to expect.

Situation C represents a third possibility. The researcher would conjure/create/find many possible price scenarios, enough to satisfactorily represent the bulk of future price scenarios, and test/optimize his method on all of them. He would then use the best overall setting in real-time trading (no more testing). The many representative possible scenarios would come from historical data and from his putting together artificially produced (but possible) new scenarios. From all these he would have both statistically enough data and data that well represents all possible situations he could face in the future. If the database of scenarios were developed well, he could have more faith in the results of optimizing his methods over these scenarios for use in real-time, than traders who have a lot (but still limited in time and market possibilities) of actual trade history! More about realism in simulations, scenario generation and testing, in Chapters 3 and 4.

ABOUT SIMULATIONS IN GENERAL

We have talked about how traders use simulations and what their trade results have been, but not about the simulations themselves or their purpose.

Simulations have been employed in many forms for many years, almost as long as man's existence. In its basic form, a simulation is a likeness. Many objects, even ideas, fit that definition. Cavemen drew stick figures to represent the likenesses of animals; painters and sculptors ply their crafts to represent life in visual form; military commanders simulate warfare on blackboards and computers; and yes, toys are the ultimate, best-known simulations of grownups' things—ranging from simple toy cars and trucks to computer-simulated sports such as Nintendo boxing and baseball.

Simulation as we think of it in commodity trading had its origin in two unrelated areas: from charting prices and overlaying strategies atop those prices; and from military war gaming. Charting goes way back to almost the time of exchange creation, when traders would chart prices and then overlay/draw formations (heads and shoulders, rounding bottoms, etc.—the early form of price prediction). Operations research began during World War II when the British developed ways of maximizing bombing effectiveness using mathematics and aerial photography.

Today many political, industrial, scientific, and military applications of simulations abound. From poll sampling to predict election results, consumer sampling on new toothpaste before major marketing, and queuing theory for traffic control, to LINK simulators for fliers, optimization of NASA payloads, and damage control predictions on supply routes in military war gaming, simulations have well proved their worth to a large variety of situations in everyday life.

For the investment world, simulations have been used to determine the effectiveness of strategies in the marketplace. From simple what-if (interest rates rose 1/2 point, e.g.) to sophisticated, totally mechanical trading, they are intended to answer the trader's questions about investment performance with his strategies.

In its simplest form (and what many people, including the author, believe is the only one needed) a simulation will measure/predict as accurately as possible what return and what risk the trader can expect from the tested strategy. This usually translates into what net profit ensues and what losses occur along the way—what he ends up with at the end and how bad losses can get during the period under scrutiny.

Many measures of performance can be examined. Table 2–1 shows a portfolio simulation with some descriptors at the top (method name, management control parameters such as initial capital, number of instruments, management fees, interest rates, etc.); a body of monthly performance figures (date, start equity, additions, withdrawls, net performances, rate of return, and NAV, or net asset value per $1,000); and a host of statistics at the bottom. Many factors are measured: profit, loss, interest, fees, statistics on trade numbers and gains/losses, gain/loss strings, profit factor, and measures of risk (Sharpe ratio, drawdowns, standard deviation of profits).

A shorter simulation output list is shown in Table 2–2. This represents a simulation of one strategy (the explosion method) on one stock (AMR) for the period 1990–95. Each row under the column headings represent the results of one particular combination of parameter values, here listed in the leftmost columns as Jobs 1–48 with variables 1, 3, 4, and 5 listed with their values. The nine pertinent simulation "barometer" statistics are total dollar profit, number of successful trades, dollars per trade profitability, the average and maximum drawdowns for the price history covered, the number of drawdowns that occurred, the average time per trade, and the profit factor (total gains divided by total losses, another measure of return and risk). Although all statistics are useful, I eventually narrow them down to total

T A B L E   2–1

Portfolio Simulation for Stock Trades

```
PORTFOLIO SIMULATION
--------------------

TRADE ALLOC=NON-RESERVE CASH/(NO. PILES *MARGIN)

COMBINED METHODS(4)-LONGS AND SHORTS

INITIAL CAPITAL=$ 10000000
NO. PILES= 80
RESERVE PCT.= 0
NO. STOCKS= 80
START,END DATES:  900101   TO   951229
TRADE STOP LEVEL(FR. OFF EQUITY PEAK)= .5
REINVESTMENT LEVEL FR.  .1
REINVESTMENT AMT FR.  1
MGMT FEE(MO.)= .0041667
INCENTIVE FEE(MO.)= .1
INT. RATE FACTOR ON TOTAL EQUITY= 0


MARGIN%= 50
COMM/SH=$ .03
MONTHLY PERFORMANCE($)
----------------------
```

YEAR/MO/DAY	STARTING EQUITY	ADDITIONS	WITHDRAWLS	NET PERFORMANCE	ENDING EQUITY	RATE OF RETURN	NAV PER $1000
900131	+10000000	+0	+0	-60678	+9939322	-0.61	+994
900231	+9939322	+0	+0	-201156	+9738166	-2.02	+974
900331	+9738166	+0	+0	-270404	+9467762	-2.78	+947
900431	+9467762	+0	+0	-198663	+9269099	-2.10	+927
900531	+9269099	+0	+0	-17849	+9251250	-0.19	+925
900631	+9251250	+0	+0	-3470	+9247780	-0.04	+925
900731	+9247780	+0	+0	-74651	+9173129	-0.81	+917
900831	+9173129	+0	+0	+830562	+10003691	+9.05	+1000
900931	+10003691	+0	+0	+934026	+10937717	+9.34	+1094
901031	+10937717	+0	+0	+94660	+11032377	+0.87	+1103
901131	+11032377	+0	+0	-488474	+10543903	-4.43	+1054
901231	+10543903	+0	+0	+149630	+10693533	+1.42	+1069
910131	+10693533	+0	+0	+1426740	+12120273	+13.34	+1212
910231	+12120273	+0	+0	+549297	+12669570	+4.53	+1267
910331	+12669570	+0	+0	+920677	+13590247	+7.27	+1359
910431	+13590247	+0	+0	-73647	-13516600	-0.54	+1352
910531	+13516600	+0	+0	+1017522	+14534122	+7.53	+1453
910631	+14534122	+0	+0	-972923	+13561199	-6.69	-1356
910731	+13561199	+0	-0	-98206	+13462993	-0.72	+1346
910831	+13462993	+0	+0	+1162872	+14625865	+8.64	+1463
910931	+14625865	+0	+0	+201577	+14827442	+1.38	+1483
911031	+14827442	+0	+0	-454966	+14372476	-3.07	+1437
911131	+14372476	+0	+0	-177002	+14195474	-1.23	+1420
911231	+14195474	+0	+0	+369674	+14565148	+2.60	+1457 *
920131	+14565148	+0	+0	+399648	+14964796	+2.74	+1496

(continues)

28

T A B L E   2–1 (continued)

920331	+15914871	+0	+0	-1035654	+14879217	-6.51	+1488
920431	+14879217	+0	+0	-942331	+13936886	-6.33	+1394
920531	+13936886	+0	+0	-186501	+13750385	-1.34	+1375
920631	+13750385	+0	+0	-85343	+13665042	-0.62	+1367
920731	+13665042	+0	+0	+89253	+13754295	+0.65	+1375
920831	+13754295	+0	+0	+196327	+13950622	+1.43	+1395
920931	+13950622	+0	+0	+1128471	+15079093	+8.09	+1508
921031	+15079093	+0	+0	+961960	+16041053	+6.38	+1604
921131	+16041053	+0	+0	+859883	+16900936	+5.36	+1690
921231	+16900936	+0	+0	+1055454	+17956390	+6.24	+1796
930131	+17956390	+0	+0	+761044	+18717434	+4.24	+1872
930231	+18717434	+0	+0	-257836	+18459598	-1.38	+1846
930331	+18459598	+0	+0	-2922	+18456676	-0.02	+1846
930431	+18456676	+0	+0	+424412	+18881088	+2.30	+1888
930531	+18881088	+0	+0	+1982966	+20864054	+10.50	+2086
930631	+20864054	+0	+0	+4121252	+24985306	+19.75	+2499
930731	+24985306	+0	+0	+843452	+25828758	+3.38	+2583
930831	+25828758	+0	+0	+934942	+26763700	+3.62	+2676
930931	+26763700	+0	+0	-722398	+26041302	-2.70	+2604
931031	+26041302	+0	+0	+1083906	+27125208	+4.16	+2713
931131	+27125208	+0	+0	-2409118	+24716090	-8.88	+2472
931231	+24716090	+0	+0	+445694	+25161784	+1.80	+2516
940131	+25161784	+0	+0	+519378	+25681162	+2.06	+2568
940231	+25681162	+0	+0	+64308	+25745470	+0.25	+2575
940331	+25745470	+0	+0	-1056224	+24689246	-4.10	+2469
940431	+24689246	+0	+0	+509262	+25198508	+2.06	+2520
940531	+25198508	+0	+0	-1364388	+23834120	-5.41	+2383
940631	+23834120	+0	+0	-265648	+23568472	-1.11	+2357
940731	+23568472	+0	+0	-118908	+23449564	-0.50	+2345
940831	+23449564	+0	+0	+902946	+24352510	+3.85	+2435
940931	+24352510	+0	+0	-515050	+23837460	-2.11	+2384
941031	+23837460	+0	+0	+937836	+24775296	+3.93	+2478
941131	+24775296	+0	+0	-589744	+24185552	-2.38	+2419
941231	+24185552	+0	+0	+423954	+24609506	+1.75	+2461
950131	+24609506	+0	+0	-432574	+24176932	-1.76	+2418
950231	+24176932	+0	+0	+480686	+24657618	+1.99	+2466
950331	+24657618	+0	+0	-137720	+24519898	-0.56	+2452
950431	+24519898	+0	+0	-168552	+24351346	-0.69	+2435
950531	+24351346	+0	+0	+81918	+24433264	+0.34	+2443
950631	+24433264	+0	+0	+358522	+24791786	+1.47	+2479
950731	+24791786	+0	+0	+1359842	+26151628	+5.49	+2615
950831	+26151628	+0	+0	-499220	+25652408	-1.91	+2565
950931	+25652408	+0	+0	+514704	+26167112	+2.01	+2617
951031	+26167112	+0	+0	-1024182	+25142930	-3.91	+2514
951131	+25142930	+0	+0	+759734	+25902664	+3.02	+2590
951229	+25902664	+0	+0	+680124	+26582788	+2.63	+2658

```
P/L STATISTICS
- - - - - - - - - - - - - -

GROSS NET PROFIT  $    +23873278
GROSS PROFIT    $    +47206784    GROSS LOSS    $   -23333506
TOTAL FEES    $    7290491      TOTAL INTEREST    $        0
```

(continues)

T A B L E   2–1 (concluded)

TOTAL INCENTIVE FEES	$ 1712521		
NET PROFIT	$ +16582787		
TOTAL # OF TRADES	838	PERCENTAGE PROFITABLE	45.7
NUMBER OF WINNING TRADES	383	NUMBER OF LOSING TRADES	455
LARGEST WINNING TRADE %	24.09	LARGEST LOSING TRADE %	-2.63
AVERAGE WINNING TRADE %	0.87	AVERAGE LOSING TRADE %	-0.41
RATIO REWARD/RISK(%)	2.1	AVG. TRADE(WIN & LOSS) %	+0.18
MAX CONSECUTIVE WINNERS	8	MAX CONSECUTIVE LOSERS	11
AVG. # BARS IN WINNERS	177.2	AVG. # BARS IN LOSERS	85.7
WORST DWDN ON TOTEQ.(% OF PK)	16.5	AVG. DWDN ON TOTEQ.(% OF PK)	3.8
PROFIT FACTOR($)	2.0	NO. DWDNS	45
AVG. MONTHLY PROFIT (%)	+1.48	STD. DEV. MO. PROFIT (%)	4.81
SHARPE RATIO	0.31		
%NET NAV / WORST DWDN	10		
%NET NAV / AVE DWDN	44		
TOTAL EXEC. COSTS =$ 1193941			

profit and average or maximum drawdown—one representing return, the other risk.

Investment simulations have the same central purpose (to predict return and risk, and other salient, related statistics) and the same general workings: Take the strategy, calculate its decisions and effects on one or more instruments, and keep track of and accurately monitor the results using a few or many measurements of the profits and losses, over a specified period of time.

TABLE 2-2

Trade Simulation Summaries for Multiple Parameter Values

DATE=9/10/96
FOR FILE AMR
EXPLOSION/GOAL METHOD-LONGS ONLY
PROG. 1001
AVE. SHS TRADED = 100
C(1)= 59.75
START, END DATES 900101 951231

TOTALS BY JOB NO.

JOB	VAR1	VAR3	VAR4	VAR5	$TOT.PROF	NO.SUCC	NO.TRADES	$PROF/TR	$AVE.DRAWDOWN	$MAXDD	NO.DWDNS	AVE. TIME/TRA	PROFIT FACTOR
1	5	1	0.10	0.50	+334	6	11	+30	313	613	3	4.5	1.3
2	5	1	0.10	0.70	+719	6	11	+65	313	613	3	4.6	1.7
3	5	1	0.10	0.90	+849	6	11	+77	313	613	3	4.6	1.9
4	5	1	0.20	0.50	+88	1	1	+88	0	0	0	5.0	100.0
5	5	1	0.20	0.70	+88	1	1	+88	0	0	0	5.0	100.0
6	5	1	0.20	0.90	+88	1	1	+88	0	0	0	5.0	100.0
19	20	1	0.10	0.50	+2133	9	13	+164	698	698	1	14.4	2.6
20	20	1	0.10	0.70	+2653	9	13	+204	506	600	2	17.5	3.0
21	20	1	0.10	0.90	+2379	8	11	+216	256	300	2	23.3	5.6
22	20	1	0.20	0.50	-13	0	1	-13	13	13	1	20.0	0.0
23	20	1	0.20	0.70	-13	0	1	-13	13	13	1	20.0	0.0
24	20	1	0.20	0.90	-13	0	1	-13	13	13	1	20.0	0.0
25	20	1	0.30	0.50	-13	0	1	-13	13	13	1	20.0	0.0
26	20	1	0.30	0.70	-13	0	1	-13	13	13	1	20.0	0.0
27	20	1	0.30	0.90	-13	0	1	-13	13	13	1	20.0	0.0
37	60	1	0.10	0.50	+936	7	11	+85	679	1650	3	37.7	1.4
38	60	1	0.10	0.70	+1338	6	11	+122	884	1531	2	49.3	1.5
39	60	1	0.10	0.90	+1373	5	10	+137	595	1397	3	52.4	1.5
40	60	1	0.20	0.50	+535	3	5	+107	1225	1225	1	40.8	1.4
41	60	1	0.20	0.70	+1300	3	5	+260	1225	1225	1	57.4	1.9
42	60	1	0.20	0.90	+959	2	4	+240	1225	1225	1	66.0	1.7
43	60	1	0.30	0.50	-1225	0	1	-1225	1225	1225	1	60.0	0.0
44	60	1	0.30	0.70	-1225	0	1	-1225	1225	1225	1	60.0	0.0
45	60	1	0.30	0.90	-1225	0	1	-1225	1225	1225	1	60.0	0.0
46	60	3	0.10	0.50	-925	0	2	-463	925	925	1	60.0	0.0
47	60	3	0.10	0.70	-925	0	2	-463	925	925	1	60.0	0.0
48	60	3	0.10	0.90	-925	0	2	-463	925	925	1	60.0	0.0

CHAPTER 3
_____

Realistic Trading Simulations

What does it mean to simulate trading?

The many types of simulations in industry, government, science, and other areas have one theme in common: to most accurately model or represent the activities studied. They may have varying degrees of detail (a gaming simulation may deal only with card counting and pack definition, but a Great Lakes Basin simulation may try to include all ecosystems down to the snail level), but they all strive to accurately, mathematically define and keep track of all (or the major) events and relationships in the model. Just like toy manufacturers try to replicate as many details and size relationships of a full-sized, real automobile in their toy car as possible, so do most simulation modelers.

The LINK flight simulator was one of the first and most lifelike simulators of our time. Built to train pilot students and retrain experienced ones (because it became so good), the flight simulator mimicked every detail of real cabins and in-flight situations—down to the instrumentation (often just taken directly from a real aircraft cabin), chairs, cabin dimensions, and even the outside of the aircraft—wind, clouds, airfield lights, other aircraft and so forth. Finally, to make it seem just like an airplane in flight, the whole training compartment was put on rollers and allowed to pitch, weave, turn, bank, and go upside down—so real it was scary!

Traders do not have quite that level of detail or realism to reproduce, unless they wish to import all or many real-life details such as weather, government actions, news, personalities, and so on, into their model.

Most trade simulations only go down to the level of price possibilities; how or why they act and perform the way they do is of no real consequence, only the result of all the outside influences on prices counts.

The trader then has only two dimensions of prices to consider: what actual prices can occur and what the probability of occurrence is for each price; and time. Rather than try to predict exact price levels at some point in time (as an exact price at some exact point in time is probably more difficult to predict than a possible price change any time) researchers look at price *changes* (or percentage price changes). Also, they are more interested in predicting cumulative price changes over time, because traders only profit by prices *changing significantly* (in their favor, naturally!).

Basically the trader has only a few major components in his trade simulator: price actions, his decision toolbox, and the housing or mechanism to translate these two into a portfolio profit-and-loss bottom line.

We talked (briefly) before about the trader's toolbox and the accounting mechanism that tracked his actions. He has certain variables at his disposal and control: initial and reinvestment monies, allocation strategies, and timing methods. Each of these topics is very important, has been addressed by many researchers and writers, and will be dealt with in detail in Chapter 5 in a unified, overview fashion. Keeping track of the portfolio is essentially an accounting function, and the subject was addressed with an adequate portfolio program in Chapter 2.

In this chapter we are most concerned with and wish to highlight price actions. They are not controllable or even easily defined, but are the single most important ingredient in the simulation formula. The trader can react to the marketplace and take best advantage of it or protect himself best against adversity and can accurately track his results, but he cannot control or influence prices, which solely make or break his investment program. If prices double each year, he stands to make fortunes; if prices stand still, he will most certainly lose (time and execution costs will kill the portfolio).

PRICE MOVEMENTS: A SHORT COURSE

There are generally three schools of thought about how prices behave. Refer to Figure 3–1 for the following discussion.

The trend school (A) popularized and adhered to by many brokers, traders, and individual speculators, holds that price movements are created

Price Models

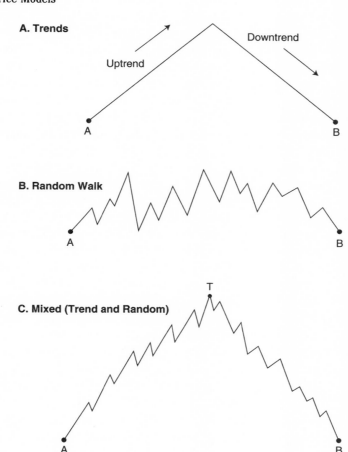

A. Trends

Uptrend

Downtrend

A

B

B. Random Walk

A

B

C. Mixed (Trend and Random)

T

A

B

and controlled by savvy or influential market participants. They believe major participants like banks, governments, fund managers or just favorable news and reports heavily and directly influence price moves, to the point where clearly discernible and large moves (trends) take place frequently. They do admit to some back and forth, mostly unchanging price patterns, which they attribute to uninfluential buying or selling by the general public.

Random walk theorists (B), mostly situated in the academic environment, hold that price changes are random and that the trends people see on charts are not real, deterministic, or caused or controlled by anyone or any group of investors, but are the cumulative effect of probabilities of price changes with more and larger upticks just happening to occur to cause an "uptrend." They do admit to the existence of long-term drift (due to inflation, population growth, and general human productivity) and occasional big events that momentarily jar prices one way or the other but that eventually settle back down into some natural trading range.

The third school is a combination of the first two: This mixed school admits to the existence of much randomness—most of the time, in fact—but does acknowledge that certain events or groups of investors/ influencers can affect prices frequently enough to cause them to move in one direction for a sustained, significant move. Essentially these adherents will agree with trend followers that the path from point A to point T in situation C is indeed a(n) (up)trend and, similarly, that the path from point T to point B also constitutes a (down)trend, but they also agree with the random walk school that much of the time the price changes between those points A, T, and B are (strictly speaking) unrelated to one another and that it is very difficult to discern ahead of time or even while they are occuring that there are indeed trends developing.

We will use both the random walk and mixed models later on for simulating price movements.

SCENARIO POSSIBILITIES

Before the trader applies or uses any of the above or other price models in a simulator, he should understand also how much—how many times—he will be applying them.

The major reason he wishes to examine many different price scenarios is that there are many possible price patterns, events, or outcomes that could occur. That is, the future will be some combination of possible price paths, due to many different causes and events. We could have one unending, unbroken upward trend because everyone works hard and cooperates well (no war—pure bliss), which is very doubtful. Similarly, doomsday could set in (war, pestilence, an earth-meteor colision, etc.) and the markets could go ceaselessly downward, to being worth almost nothing (also very doubtful). More likely, a mix will occur: good and bad events, up and down trends, sprinkled with many indeterminable price movements (sideways, back-and-forth price action).

In our simulations we have to plan for many different possible price scenarios so we can determine how our trading strategies will fare.

In most simulations, practictioners include possible outcomes or states of the model they are simulating (traffic flow; space satellite; and, here, the investment markets) and find out the result of each. These results are then weighted and combined into a final "average" outcome, and/or probabilities are computed for particular scenarios or groups of events. For example, a traffic model would output the average queue time at a bridge or tunnel, with probabilities of getting through the line under X or over Y minutes. In the market models, we would look for average return (total dollars profit, say) and/or risk (worst or average cumulative losing dollar string) during the typical period of time projected, for example, and perhaps probabilities of making more than X dollars or incurring less than Y dollars risk. Of course, many other statistics and probabilities can be sought (see Tables 2–1 and 2–2 for some possible statistics).

At the heart of the model are the possible price scenarios: If there is only one, then it doesn't take much simulating to find out the results. But the real world is quite different; there are literally zillions (more than billions) of possible price scenarios in real life.

Figure 3–2 gives a *very* brief picture of some price scenarios gold could experience in a year's time. Prices could move from A to B (an uptrend), or from A to C (a downtrend). There are many places gold prices could end up. (A couple of possibilities, B and C, are shown here, but there are many others—500 possible changes per day with 255 trading days in the year.)

More important, there are many ways or *paths* it could take just to get to B or C alone. In fact, if we mix the end point and interim path(s), gold has the following number of possible distinctly different paths it could take in one year's time:

$$\text{Number of paths gold/1 year} = (500)^{255}$$
$$= \text{A very big number}$$

This is arrived at by toting up the number of possible close to close price changes in a day ($.10 or 1 dime is the smallest possible change; it could change up $+.30 or $2.40, or down –$1.20, say up to a maximum

FIGURE 3-2

Possible Gold Scenarios for One Year: (500)^{250}

(Close Price Changes Only)

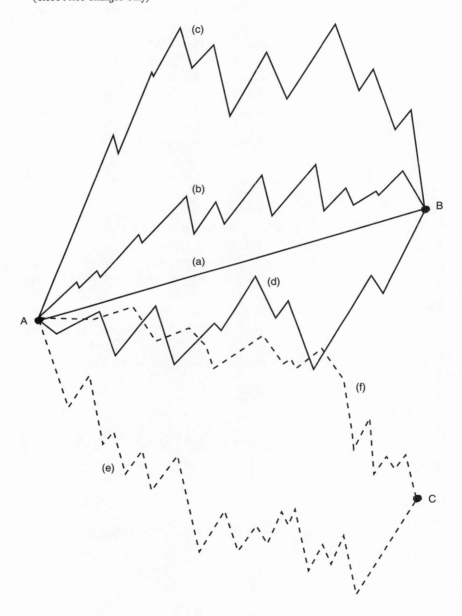

of +\$25.00 and a minimum of –\$25.00), which total 250 of positive changes of .1 plus 250 of negative changes of –.1 = 500 possible changes. Each day is independent of the next (we are quoting the random walk school here), so the whole year's number of trading days (255) must factor in. From probability theory we apply the formula

$$\text{Number of paths gold/1 year} = 500 \times 500 \times 500 \times 500 \ldots \times 500$$
$$\text{(Day 1) (Day 2) (Day 3)}$$
$$\text{(Day 4) } \ldots \text{ (Day 255)}$$
$$= (500)^{255}$$

This number becomes enormous because each day's close change action (500 possibilities) is now combined with each of the next day's possible changes (again 500), to create 25,000 possibilities after only two days of price movements.

Though this is staggering, it gets even worse when you realize we have not accounted for the possible combinations of open, high, and low prices! (And they may be independent and multiplicative combinations with close to close changes!).

What these price change combinations do is alert the trader to the many price paths *possible*, only a few of which (5,10, 20 years) he has seen or researched. Past history is but a tiny, tiny fraction of the awesome number of possible price scenarios! Worse than that, we probably conjecture that those exact scenarios (day to day price change relationships) will not repeat, so we are looking for many zillions of possible *new* ones. Some stocks/commodities (like S & P and currencies) have virtually no limits to daily price movements, which makes the number of paths per year even larger!

Why are we so concerned with price *paths,* and not simply with where prices end up at the close of a period? After all, if a trend-following method is simulated, isn't the net profit related to the period end, the end of the trend? No. Prices could wildly gyrate up and down, whipsawing the trend method back and forth with losses, even though the final price ebbed quite a bit (up or down) from the beginning price. Conversely, the period start and end prices could be the same, but big (smooth or wildly volatile) gyrations could have occurred in between, giving many a method plenty of profit opportunities.

Without question, it is the *path,* or how prices gyrate and meander and get to one place from another, that determines not only profit potential but how a particular method will fare. Whipsaw markets give plenty of profit opportunities to contrary methods, while they hurt trend-following ones badly. Each method is sensitive and set up to deal with usually only one type of price market or set of patterns, so the path prices take is extremely important. And if there are many thousands or millions or zillions of paths, the trader better test his method on all or at least a good, representative sampling to find out how it will fare on future possibilities.

SCENARIO PROBABILITIES AND PRICE SIMULATION PLANNING

There are a lot (zillions) of possible price paths or scenarios for every investment vehicle, which must be considered and evaluated with a trader's method in a simulated environment. But the number can be whittled down, using common sense, expert judgment, and some help from statistics.

First, a review of probabilities and possible price path outcomes will help crystallize path analysis and possible price scenarios facing the trader in the future.

BASIC COMBINATIONS: PRICE CHANGE ORDERING AND MAGNITUDES

Prices move only in two directions, up(+) or down(−). Strings of price changes will be mixtures of up and down changes. Two up in a row can occur as frequently as two down in a row; or up then down; or down then up.

If we don't care about the order of change, many sequences can be considered the same. But we *do* care, because methods look at price changes in *sequence,* the order in which they occur: A sequence of three ups followed by three downs may mean something quite different to our timing method than a string of up then down, up then down, up then down (see Figure 3–3). When we eliminate scenarios that are or seem duplicative, we will have to be careful to not exclude those that have even slight but key differences (in price change order or in magnitude—see below).

The magnitude of price changes (see Figure 3–3, situation 2) will also make a difference: obviously a 10-percent change will have more effect on most timing methods than a 1-percent change.

It turns out price changes are normally distributed with an average for many markets near zero, but for some the mean is significantly positive. The stock market has had for many years an average increase of around 9 percent, reflecting mostly inflation, which in turn reflects popu-

FIGURE 3–3

Key Components of Price Changes

1. Order/Sequence

a. Three ups followed
    by three downs

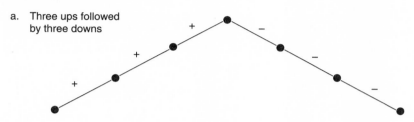

b. Three pairs of
    ups and downs

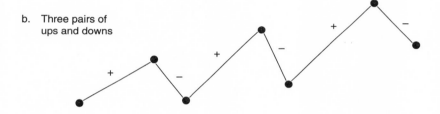

2. Magnitude

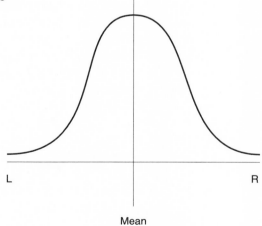

lation growth and productivity. This means there are many price changes, plus and minus, that are small, a moderate number of moderate-sized changes, and few that are large.

From the above discussion about ordering and magnitudes, and from much research, it turns out that trend moves (a long sequence of large net price change) should occur fairly infrequently. But in the real world, these moves occur more frequently and are of larger magnitudes than price distribution and random ordering would dictate.

PRICE MODELS

In real life, natural and (especially) human events seem to continue to disrupt the financial world more often than randomness would predict.

It would be nice to have omniscience, to know ahead exactly what tomorrow's *Wall Street Journal* would read, but barring that unlikelihood, perhaps we could develop more accurate models that call for better descriptions of price movements. In the context of the two above price movement descriptions—order and magnitude of price changes—maybe we could improve one or the other, or a combination of both.

It comes down to better describing the natural/normal/typical (and untypical, too) ways that prices behave. There are a number of price behavior models that could be chosen. The models range from the seemingly simplest (but hard to program and test)—charting, which describes complex price formations such as head and shoulders, rounding bottoms, flags, and gaps; to the purely academic—the random walk model, which randomly picks price changes from the normal distribution just described in Figure 3–3 (part 2, Magnitude) and strings them randomly in a sequence.

In between are models that traders/researchers believe better mirror the intentions/actions of investors. At one extreme are the modelers who see very specific influences carrying through a few days to over long periods, weeks to months: candlestick theory emphasizes individual, short-term actions and natural events, while Elliot wave depicts long-term trends having specific price milestones along the way and at the end.

At the other end of the spectrum are general price theories that loosely describe the general flow of prices: sinusoidal waves simply account for and predict the amplitude (magnitude) and frequency of up and down cycles; the Dow theory generally describes major trends (by magnitude only) and two sets of price movements embedded within the major trends (minor trends and daily movements), which can be used to predict when major trends will occur; and price vector models, describe price change runs as bull or bear moves and price trends as the cumulative of net bull and bear moves.

Several of the more representative and useful models will be explained and applied in the following chapter.

MODEL TEST DESIGN

Returning to the question of modeling price scenarios, the staggering number of price scenarios can be reduced by applying three screens or filters. Refer to Figure 3–4 for the following discussion.

The first pass or screen involves common sense. Many of the computer-generated scenarios (when we do get around to designing that plan) will come out very similar (especially with huge numbers generated), with seemingly only a price change separating them in (graphical or tabular) appearance. Unless the trader's method is extremely sensitive to any changes, he can then eliminate very similar scenarios. Care must be taken to not jettison scenarios that differ by only a few but large or crucial price changes, lest trade simulation results get skewed by omitting the seeming duplicate. After all, computer runs are cheap and fast, so better to err on the side of scenario inclusion rather than omission.

In part 1 of the figure, the two scenarios differ by .01 in the second price change, which for most timing methods will not make much difference. Note that price change order is still important: had the order been different for scenario b, and price changes 2 and 3 were interchanged, the timing method applied to that scenario might indeed have given truly different answers than for scenario a.

The trader should make sure he does not leave out scenarios that are typical and that as a group are wide ranging and represent the entire scope of price scenarios. (See part 2). This can be done by picking at least one of each major, distinct type of overall event: a large upmove with low or moderate volatility; one or more sideways move scenarios (perhaps one with high volatility, and another with low volatility); and a large net downmove, again with small or moderate volatility.

In this way he will 'box' or define the major scenarios that he will face in the future. The trader may not have all gradations in between (moderate trends, e.g.), but if he has enough scenarios (statistically speak-

FIGURE 3-4

Model Test Design: Reducing/Specifying Price Scenarios

1. Eliminate Near-Duplicate Scenarios

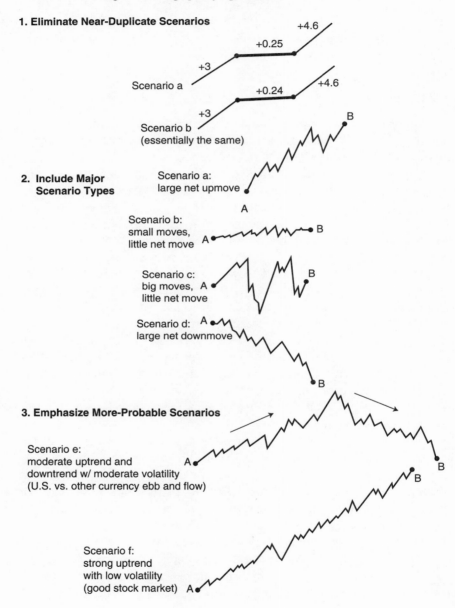

Scenario a

Scenario b
(essentially the same)

2. Include Major Scenario Types

Scenario a:
large net upmove

Scenario b:
small moves,
little net move

Scenario c:
big moves,
little net move

Scenario d:
large net downmove

3. Emphasize More-Probable Scenarios

Scenario e:
moderate uptrend and
downtrend w/ moderate volatility
(U.S. vs. other currency ebb and flow)

Scenario f:
strong uptrend
with low volatility
(good stock market)

ing, probably a minimum of 100), he can draw significant conclusions after his timing and portfolio testing are completed.

Finally, referring to part 3 of the figure, an experienced trader may wish to emphasize certain scenario types, and to deemphasize others, to make his scenario portfolio more precise and his simulations more accurate and powerful. This would be particularly more relevant if he were concentrating on one or more specific markets. In this example, the trader has more experience and feels that two types of markets will greatly predominate: a two-sided market like currencies, which have both up and down trends occurring that are typically moderate in size and volatility; and a strong uptrend for the stock market and stocks he follows, with low volatility. If he is prophetic, his timing simulations will be right on target and his trading results extremely accurate. But he had better be sure that these markets will occur and predominate, otherwise the resulting trade simulation could greatly overstate the net profits and even the risk statistics.

OVERALL PORTFOLIO PLAN

Price scenario generation is but one, albeit very important, part of the complete portfolio plan. A detailed, in-depth discussion of this principal part of the plan will be presented in Chapter 5.

Selection of trading vehicles or instruments is another important part. If the trader chooses across the board (includes most instruments) he will be able to reduce risk generally in the portfolio, but at the cost of perhaps lesser returns or profits. A selection of just a few instruments or just one instrument (gold, say) could give him spectacular returns (e.g., skyrocketing prices to $800 per ounce) or very mundane gains or even substantial losses (shrinking or listless gold prices during the late 1980s and early 1990s), definitely increasing the risk factor and leading to unknown profits (unless he is absolutely sure).

Timing methods also play a very important role. Some methods do poorly or well in certain markets (moving averages do great in large trended times, poorly in choppy markets), and typically the trade results are highly dependent upon what price scenarios exist.

Return-and-risk analysis portfolio tuning to reflect price scenario reality and the trader's desires can be accomplished when all these elements are combined into portfolio runs. The trader can change some portfolio management variables (reinvestment rates, inclusion/exclusion of different instruments, cash reserve, etc.) and rerun the portfolio for risk-and-return analyses.

The overall plan is detailed in Chapter 5.

CHAPTER 4

Price Scenario Generation

Our goal is to produce price scenarios that accurately reflect the full panorama of the future for an instrument. This will mean generating enough scenarios (hundreds, thousands, etc.) to be both statistically valid and fully representative (all major outcomes are included) for testing and analyzing timing and portfolio models.

There are two main elements of the price scenario generation model: choosing appropriate period(s) in order to accurately represent the main/all possible conditions; and choosing the price model itself—the variables and their relationship, and how prices are generated to produce different scenarios.

In this chapter we will address aspects of picking past representative periods; price models; price generation mechanisms; and a plan to put these elements together to generate fully representative price scenarios. Many examples will be given.

CHOOSING PAST PERIODS

It is easy to say "pick a period that well represents the future." That is very much like the question "which comes first, the chicken or the egg". If we knew exactly the period that will likely repeat, we could test and analyze our methods on just that period and be done with it.

There is no question that picking a period for method test purposes is an (and some would definitely say *the* most) important aspect of a trade simulation. However, one should be careful not to fall into the trap of believing that a particular period will be the sole representative time slot, both in length and exact characteristics (same price order from day to day) that the trader will see in the future.

On the other hand, we are only looking for some *general* characteristics and some specific examples of types of markets. Our scenario generator will do the rest: put together all sorts of combinations of prices up and down, patterns, and so forth.

For example, if the trader believes that for stock A only uptrends will occur in the future, with an average rise of 10 percent per year (about the same as the general market), he will look for examples of these two stipulations (upwards direction and 10 percent per year magnitude) in past history. Of course, this is a very crude or general set of requirements, which allows many historical years to qualify and allows all sorts of other traits to occur (high or low price volatility, all sorts of different price formations and dependencies, and different price levels).

A serious question, from a mathematical viewpoint, always arises: Does the trader get very specific in his requirements for historical representation of the future (such as specifying particular price events, their occurence in time, exact trend lengths, etc.), which is known in mathematics as a *strong condition;* or does he become very general, with as little specifics as possible, leaving only a few general types of markets to simulate (known as the *weak case* in mathematics, although ironically it allows more general, sweeping conclusions or applications to occur).

Unfortunately there is no easy answer. This is where the skill, expertise, and confidence of the trader/researcher enters in. If he is absolutely convinced that gold will be in a sustained, strong uptrend hereinafter, he will look for such periods in the past, generate price scenarios based on those periods, and live (die) by his confident choice. The price generation model does not judge his choice; it simply reflects his dictum of past history. But because he chose this 'strong" historical case, his scenarios will be narrowly and strongly reflective of this choice. He may be quite right, in which case his future trades will look smashingly great. But his price scenarios and subsequent trading results could be way off the mark because his representative period was not that at all. As they say in the computer business, garbage in, garbage out.

I tend to gravitate towards the more general (weak mathematically) approach: represent as many situations as possible, but stay general, letting the computer and the price models generate many interesting scenario possibilities. It is probably better to model more possibilities and err that some (especially bad trade producing ones) will not show up in the future, than to bet on only a few very specific price events (e.g., a strong uptrend) and be unpleasantly surprised when some events not modeled also or only show up (e.g., a sharp downtrend for our gold bug).

For these reasons I would try to construct general situations that cover the most broad occurrences (e.g., trends and no trends) and include all sorts of examples of minor characteristics, such as price volatility (magnitude or size of price changes, not the direction). Of course, this means identifying major and minor characteristics of prices over periods of time.

Time Considerations

The first stipulation must be the period size and time increments. The time increment is usually an easy choice: Most traders trade/act on a daily basis, although many act weekly (for the stock markets), others (e.g., pension fund managers) look at monthly and quarterly figures, while at the other extreme fast speculators examine 15-minute and even tick-by-tick charts. Period size is a tougher call because it must encompass all possible price events and some that are large in duration (e.g., long-term trends). Also, it should probably be pegged at the same length of time managers and clients examine in order to review/analyze trade results (typically one year). I would generally stipulate a year or less for commodities and other faster-paced and more-leveraged markets; and one to five years for stocks and other markets that reflect longer-term general market and economic trends.

Price Characteristics

What type of price characteristics should the trader seek to incorporate/encompass in his chosen period time frame? Again, the chicken and egg argument comes up because one must know what his price model (see later discucssion) will look for and mimic. But it is at this point the trader must identify the different event possibilities (and then later propose, develop, and use a proper price model that will incorporate all of those events) that he could face in the future. Luckily, with some price models he will use (see later discussion) it is not necessary to be extremely detailed or particular about the event, especially the larger or more encompassing it is (e.g., a general uptrend is only a drift of net positive prices from time A to later time B: no stipulations are made about how long it took, its size, or particular up and down price sequence or ordering).

Some researchers might argue that too general a description could lead to very little richness in price event creation or to sharp differences in events. But it is really up to the price model—how it defines/encompasses events, whether it is too limited or indeed can produce a rich, full set of price events. (More later on price models.) So it is up to the researcher to postulate and list all the (major) types of events and let the computer/model go to work and fill in the many details and possible price events.

Figure 4–1 depicts many (perhaps not all) possible general price events. Over the period of historical and future times the trader could face uptrend, downtrend, and generally sideways markets, with varying degrees (sizes) of each. A second level of detail is how these general, period-long events happened: easily, with much certainty (low price volatility, or prices heading in the ultimate direction of period end); or with difficulty and much uncertainty (high price volatility, or prices heading strongly up and down with no clear path or direction). This makes for six possible combinations of drift–no drift, low–high volatility events (two trend states and one no-trend state in combination with these two volatility states).

Of course, there may be many subevents such as chart formations, Elliot waves, or total randomness (uncertain direction and magnitude each day) that our researcher may want to include. He must be careful, though, to not be too specific (exact types and numbers of more specific events) lest he become like the gold bug—paint himself into a corner and not allow for any surprises.

Examples of several of these general price scenarios are found in Charts 4–1 through 4–4 for American Airlines. The first shows a long-term downtrend on a monthly time basis chart, when prices fall from 45 to 10 in a steady, slowly varying downward march. That is one possible future scenario. A good model could mix up the price path, showing a sideways/up move followed by a torrential, straight drop, followed by a slightly rising trend at the end—or many other path possibilities. But the main thing is to "mix" the various price change combinations to arrive at different paths to the same (inevitable) ending, a strong drop.

FIGURE   4-1

Some Types of Price Scenarios

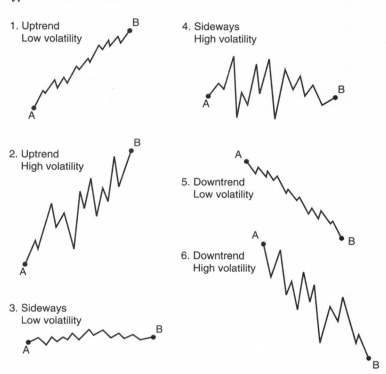

1. Uptrend
   Low volatility

2. Uptrend
   High volatility

3. Sideways
   Low volatility

4. Sideways
   High volatility

5. Downtrend
   Low volatility

6. Downtrend
   High volatility

An essentially sideways market with great up and down price volatility is depicted in Chart 4–2. Prices start and end at around 13, but drop to 9 and rise to 19 before ending up unchanged. Other price (generated) scenarios could easily include a straight uptrend to 19 then streaking prices to 12. Or the other way around: a drop to 9 or lower followed by a rise to 19, then a drop to 13, similar to what actually happened. Throw in some randomly generated price events that look like head and shoulders or rounding bottom formations, and you have many of the price patterns possible to test timing and portfolio methods.

Chart 4–3 details a strong uptrend with high volatility, completing the possible (general) price events for this stock. Again, a number of variations could be generated by a good price scenario model: a straight

CHART 4-1

Downtrend—Low Volatility

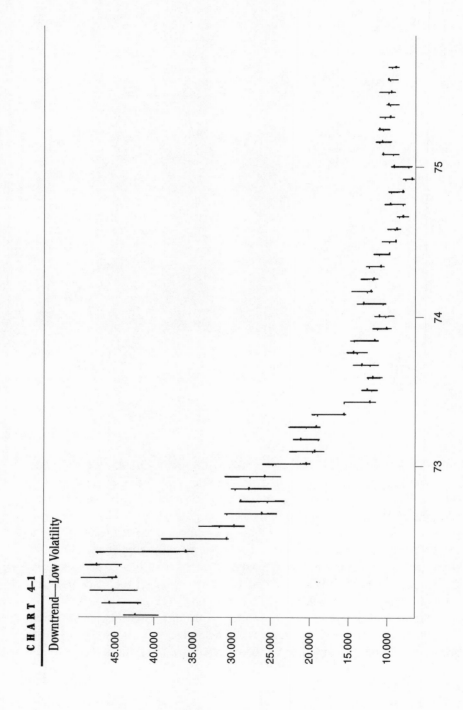

Sideways—High Volatility

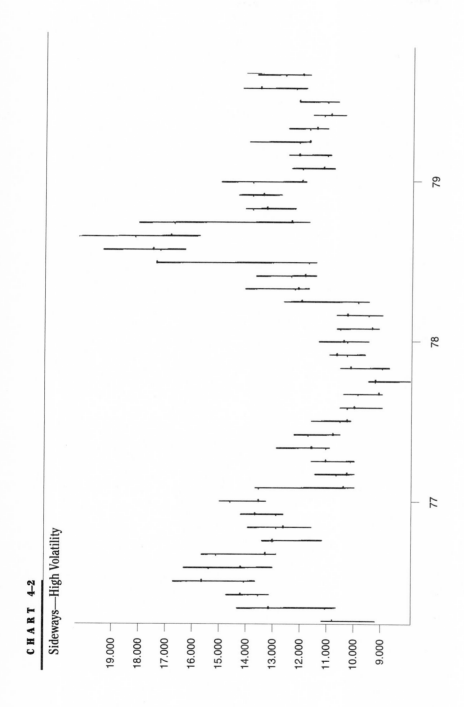

CHART 4-3

Uptrend—High Volatility

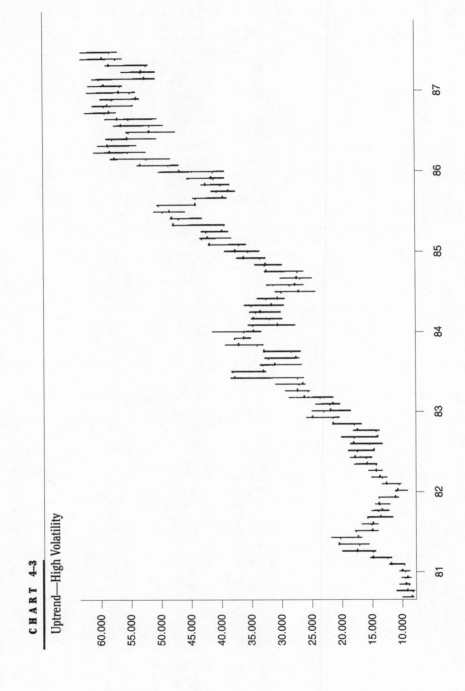

CHART 4–4

Downtrend—Low Volatility (1994)

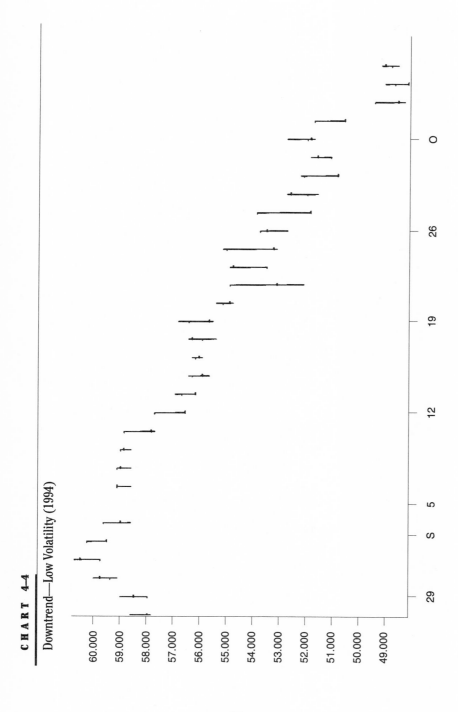

uptrend followed by a short downtrend to the eventual price of 60. Or, a slight drop to under 10 could initially happen, followed by a straight upshot to 60.

Chart 4–4 depicts a situation similar to the price trend in Chart 4–1, a steady, less-volatile downtrend, but timed on a daily basis. The different time frame will produce moves of lesser magnitude per unit time but retain many of the frequency and general-trend, no-trend, volatile, non-volatile characteristics of the larger time frames.

CHOOSING PRICE MODELS

Next on the agenda, and just as important as choosing proper periods from the past to represent elements of the future, is the proper selection and use of a price model.

A price model relates price variables to one another and to time, the unspoken (and most important) variable in the model. The relationships can be simple (close price equals low price + 1 point) or complex (some higher order partial differential equation involving not only the other price variables but compounds of them, and involving many past time values). They can be deterministic (the open price is exactly last night's close plus 2 points) or probabilistic (the close will be somewhere between high and low price, with 50 possible price points, each with equal probability of occurring). Most important, though, a good price model reflects and predicts accurately what prices will do, how they will behave.

There are two levels of accuracy: the highest is perfection, where every period's exact price relationship, magnitudes, and order of occurrence is predicted and 100 percent accuracy is called for; the second is approximation, where major features (such as trends, choppy markets, their proportionate mix, other price formations, etc.) are well represented in the results, and basic relationships (close price higher than low, but the open could and will be higher and lower than the close at different times) are always accurate. The first is omniscience, having tomorrow's *Wall Street Journal* today, and is possessed by only One. The second, for all the rest of us, means the model will approximate and represent plausible future outcomes as well as those of the past.

Price models come in many shades but generally are of two camps: the little-is-predictable and the much-is-predictable advocates. Refer to Figure 4–2 for discussion of various schools of modeling.

FIGURE 4–2

The Price Model Schools

1. Minimum Prediction

Random walk: price change magnitudes/probabilities

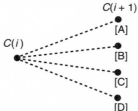

2. Specific Statistic/Event

Moving average: price direction (a)
and magnitude (b)

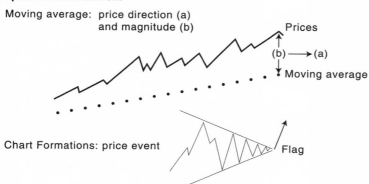

Chart Formations: price event

3. Related Events

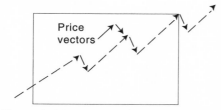

Uptrend of *M* magnitude lasting *N* days

In between are those who use various tools to discover and predict only one or a few aspects of price movements. Situation 2 in Figure 4–2 depicts the "special statistic/event" school of price models. Traders use moving averages to approximate where prices are, and they assume that is where prices should be in the short run; but more important, they use the averages to approximate the direction (differences of last-actual versus moving average) of where they are going. They take positions based on significant moves of current prices versus the average as precursors of future movement. Chartists use lines and curves on charts to construct or "engineer" various complex price formations as having taken or in the act of taking place. These constructs are predictors of other like events, and these traders will take positions long or short depending upon the direction and amount of price movement predicted.

Many brokers, traders, and academics hold to the minimal prediction school, situation 1 in Figure 4–2. They hold that price change, the single most important statistic to examine, is the only one that is at all predictable, and it is only predictable in a probabilistic sense: A change of x percent has a y percent chance of occurring, and that is that. (It is also not influenced by prior price changes at all, which lead many to conclude that trends, the accumulation of many like-sign price changes, do not occur very often and are not predictable over time.)

The third camp is relatively new and calls for a blend of the two other camps: Certain events are somewhat predictable and related but cannot be detected or predicted well until partially underway, and all events are probabilistic (cannot be accurately predicted with respect to time). A trend's existence may be detected and its eventual magnitude predicted with a certain degree of accuracy. The minimum prediction school would say there is no trend, and no change in magnitude can be accurately predicted, and the specific event school would call for a most certain price move in the next few days only.

EXAMPLES OF THREE MODELS

The three models below represent the main thinking on price relationships by the academic world and a major school of market participants who see more price relationship predictability than do those of the academic school.

The Random Walk Model

Researchers long ago (before the turn of the twentieth century a French options expert, Bachelier, started this line of thinking) proposed that price change is the relevant statistic to examine and on which to build future price scenarios rather than price levels. Osborne later proposed (from physics, Brownian motion) a working price change relationship, and Mandelbrot and Fama tested various price data and concluded that one could replicate and approximate the past with certain price change distributions. Researchers and traders have combined these representations with random selection computer techniques to build price scenarios.

The main function of the (any) model is to reproduce or manufacture prices that well approximate past price values over time and that could build plausible values in the future. We use mathematical formulas and computer devices to generate such series. Refer to Figure 4–3 for discussion of construction of these price series.

Basically the model acknowledges price changes from close to close as the principal relationship and calls for those changes to be described by or generated from a (normal) distribution or from value possibilities shown in the bottom half of the figure. The researcher would essentially go back in time and for the past period chosen collect and tabulate all close to close price changes, then build up a distribution or graph of these, marked by size on the x-axis and frequency of occurrence on the y-axis. The values would be grouped into "cells" that had equal numbers of values in them.

If there were 100 days worth of close price changes, the researcher would first order the price changes from largest to smallest, and then might choose 5 as the number of values for each cell and thus there would be 20 cells of 5 price change values each. (The rule is to have enough cells—a minimum of 20 is often stipulated—and a large enough number of values in each cell—5 usually a minimum—to assure statistical accuracy.) Then he would average the value for each cell.

He also has to collect other price change statistics—high minus close and close minus low values for each day—and tabulate cell values for them separately, as he did for the close to close price changes.

To generate prices, the researcher might use the following formulas and computer-generated random numbers in the following manner:

$C(i+1) = C(i) + \text{chg}CC$ [next close price]

$H(i+1) = C(i+1) + \text{chg}HC$ [next high price]

$L(i+1) = C(i+1) - \text{chg}CL$ [next low price]

$O(i+1) = L(i+1) + \text{chg}O * [H(i+1) - L(i+1)]$

FIGURE 4-3

The Random Walk Price Model

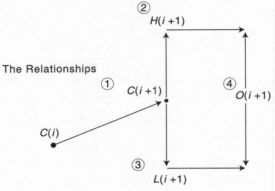

The Relationships

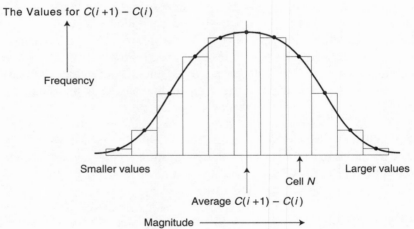

where

chg*CC* = One of the close to close price change cell values chosen randomly by the computer

chg*HC* = One of the high to close price change cell values, also chosen randomly by the computer

chg*CL* = One of the close to low price change cell values, likewise chosen randomly by the computer

chg*O* = One of the cells containing an average fraction (0 to 1.0) of the high to low price range that is open to low price, again chosen randomly. For example, the first cell might have an average fraction of .01, the fifth cell value of .13, and so on, fraction of the high-to-low range.

and

$R(i)$ = Random number varying between 0 and 1.0 with equal probability; the number is generated by the computer and is used to pick and be regenerated for each cell for all of the above formulas.

As a practical matter, when the computer generates a random number between 0 and 1.0, the price simulator will take that number and assign the corresponding average cell value for chgCC, then regenerate another random number and pick chgHC and then do the same for chg*CL*.

Example: If the random number generated by the computer were 0.152346 and there were 20 cells with various averages, the computer would choose the fourth cell and use its average value for chg*CC*. In other words, the first cell is assigned random number values 0 to .0499999 . . . , the second .05 to .099999 . . . , the third .10 to .1499999 . . . , the fourth .15 to .19999 . . . (its pick in this example), and so on. The random number would be regenerated over again for each formula (chg*HC*, for example, the next generated variable on the list) and for each new point in time (e.g., day).

The formulas were developed using the following assumptions: the close tomorrow [$C(i+1)$] will be only related to today's close [$C(i)$] and a randomly generated price change (chg*CC*). Prices in the future would thus be an assemblage of randomly generated price changes, each independent of each other, and therefore prices would be independent of each other also.

Trends and other complex, related price structures would not, in theory, exist, but could occur just from chance happening, with little probability of occurring and without being at all predictable (because they were randomly created).

To complete the picture, we need to develop high, low, and open price relationships, bearing in mind the assumption that prices are not related. The easiest and most natural relationship is to mimic the close to close formula. This is done for the next high, low, and open formulas (the high being always higher than the close, the low lower, and the open somewhere between the high and the low).

See the succeeding section for examples of generated random walk model prices.

The Sequential Walk Model

The above random walk model is a standard and will be used and tested later on, but it is weak from a "real life" modeling standpoint. Prices do not jump from close to close, and certainly not from the close to the high for the same day.

A more authentic one would model the normal, real course or sequence of trading events. The auction markets are sequential in time and move from yesterday's close to today's open, then to high and low prices within the day's trading hours, then finally to the day's close.

Thus, it would be more appropriate (see Figure 4–4) to define price relationships as

$$O(i+1) = C(i) + \text{chg}OC$$

$$H(i+1) = O(i) + \text{chg}HO$$

$$L(i+1) = O(i) - \text{chg}OL$$

$$C(i+1) = L(i) + \text{chg}C * [H(i + 1)] - L(i + 1))$$

where

chgOC = One of the current open minus prior close cell values, chosen randomly by the computer (could be a positive or negative cell value)

chgHO = One of the current high minus current open cell values, also chosen randomly by the computer (always a positive value)

chgOL = One of the current open minus current low cell values, also chosen randomly by the computer (always a positive value)

chg$C$ = One of the cell's values, also chosen randomly by the computer, with average cell value an average of close

FIGURE 4-4

The Sequential Walk Model

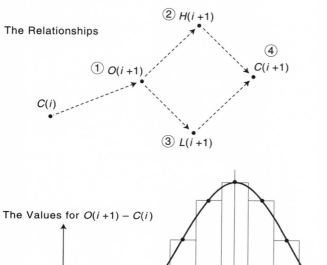

The Relationships

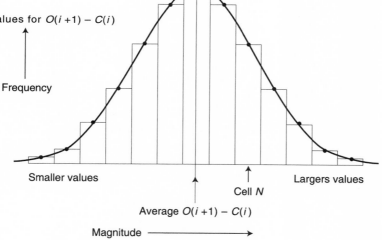

The Values for $O(i+1) - C(i)$

minus low, divided by high minus low, which is a fraction ranging between 0 and 1.0

$R(i)$ = Random number generated by the computer, varying between 0 and 1 with equal probability for each decimal number

We will also have examples of these distributions and price generations in succeeding sections.

The Price Vector Model

A common complaint that traders bring up is that chart figures are not scientific, are too interpretative, and do not really model the buying and selling forces in the market, while random walk models constitute both too simple and rigid a relationship (close-to-close price changes do not reflect more-complex, longer-term interacting forces and events, and the close to close change is not the fundamental statistic to examine; see the prior sequential walk model for one possible modification).

Traders understand it is impossible and probably not important to model every influence or price nuance in the marketplace, but rather to model more major, complex, net price activity.

From a physics viewpoint, one can posit only three independent variables in the trading place: bull or buying forces; bear or selling forces making their presence felt in positive (bull) or negative (bear) price changes; and time (refer to my book *Commodity Profits through Trend Trading,* Wiley, New York, 1982, for a thorough discussion of this model).

We are interested in the extent of buying and selling forces' influence and their net effects, not in day-to-day closing changes or other related price relationships. A buying wave, once started, often lasts more than one day. Random walk models would cut that major event to only one day arbitrarily. Also, we know buying and selling will alternate, as natural profit taking and incipient short taking try to end strong rallies. As in physics where there are countervailing forces, we are interested in the net move of the two forces, after the dust settles, so to speak.

Figure 4–5 depicts a general, strong up market, but there are a number of down days sprinkled throughout that convince a random walk model that the strong move was just a series of low-probability coincidences of random upticks, not a real caused event. Similarly, at point (1), moving averages might have gotten trapped going short, as prices were dipping sharply below the longer-term averages and signaling a downtrend.

If we instead regard every price change with the same sign and in sequence as being part of a larger price move in the same direction and net out the next counter-sign move, we would in effect be looking at the (physics) resultant of two (bull and bear) forces and could then regard this as the building block of price moves, not close to close price changes, which have no physical or financial relevance.

FIGURE 4-5

The Price Vector Price Model

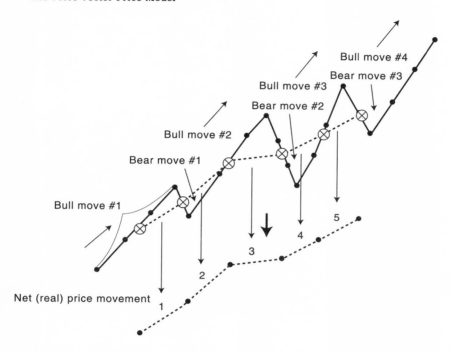

In Figure 4–5 bull move #1 spans two price changes, while bear move #1 consists of only one. Bull move #2 occurs over three price changes, and likewise for bear move #2.

If we were to "net out" bull move #1 and bear move #1 (one legitimate way is to join the midpoints of the bull and bear moves) we would end up with a line between the first two (leftmost) circled Xs. Transpose that segment, net move #1, down to the net price vector graph below and circle the number 1. Moving on to net move #2, this consists of joining the midpoints of bear move #1 and bull move #2 and bringing it down onto the second vector graph as net move #2 (circled). If we continue the process, we end up with a smooth, continuous, ever-rising string of net moves, to form an uptrend. Note (statisticians) that there is no smoothing, as in moving averages.

The result of filtering out/dissecting the original price changes to net price movement is the clear identification of major price moves and an accurate model of the major forces and their effects in the marketplace. While price *change* correlations over large sets of data turn out to calculate near zero, perhaps only .02, indicating no statistical relationship between price *changes* (the random walk model basic premise), correlations run on this model's net price moves show values closer to 0.4 as an average, on many time frames and instruments tested.

Data Collection for the Price Vector Model

The first step in constructing a price vector model is to collect and tally price data properly. Figure 4–6 displays the main ingredients of a simple version of the price vector model. This basic version simulates the bull (up) price moves and bear (down) price moves as separate items, with prices generated in "strings" or basically for each (bull or bear) move.

The first task is to identify and catalog the price vectors as bull (up) or bear (down). The first calculation involves finding out how many there are of each (up and down separately) and then graphing them separately by number of segments or price changes for each vector or move (e.g., up vector #1 has two price changes, up vector #4 has five, #7 has three price changes, and so on). We will develop graphs that first arrange/rank them by size (many will be together, two or three price changes each, for example), then divide the ranked ones into a number of cells (at least 10, preferably 20 or more) containing equal numbers of vectors/upmoves, then calculate each cell's average value. The resultant graphs are shown, for upvectors and downvectors separately, in Figure 4–6, case 1). We will call these (price vector) segment distribution graphs.

We will need another set of graphs, this time to find out how many vectors there were, then how many cells there should be for each piece or segment (price change) in these vectors. When we do construct price vectors, we will piece them together (vector) segment by segment, and assume that each segment will reflect *different* historical instances. The first price change in an upvector may have typically been a robust mover, with high and close prices very strong compared with other price changes later on and near the end of the (bull) price move.

Figure 4–6, case 2 shows a simple graph of number of vectors versus segment number. This should be understood to mean how many vectors (y-axis) have at least the number of segments chartered on the x-axis.

F I G U R E   4–6

Simple Price Vector Model—Data Collection

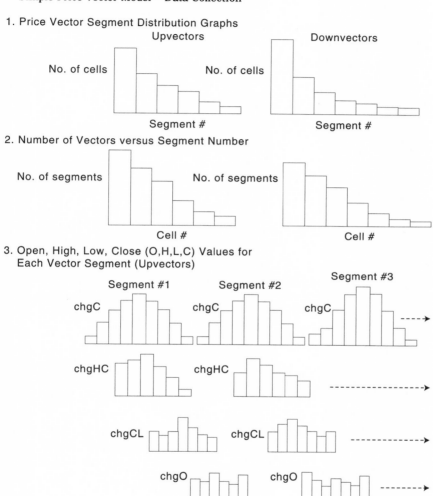

1. Price Vector Segment Distribution Graphs

Upvectors

No. of cells

Segment #

Downvectors

No. of cells

Segment #

2. Number of Vectors versus Segment Number

No. of segments

Cell #

No. of segments

Cell #

3. Open, High, Low, Close (O,H,L,C) Values for
   Each Vector Segment (Upvectors)

Segment #1   Segment #2   Segment #3

chgC   chgC   chgC

chgHC   chgHC

chgCL   chgCL

chgO   chgO

There may be 97 up-price vectors in a year's period for the Japanese yen, each of which had at least two segments in them (two price changes), 52 that had at least three segments, and so on.

The third and final group of graphs is a series of graphs running horizontally, one set for each (daily) close, high, low, and open price changes.

(We will use the random walk model to construct prices for each day or segment; see prior discussion for the formulas and explanations.)

The first (leftmost) graph is a distribution graph just as constructed for the random walk data previously discussed, separately for upvectors and for downvectors. The researcher goes back over the time period in question and collects the close-to-close price changes for the *first* segment/price change of each upvector, cumulates this information, and puts it into the form of the distribution graph of Figure 4–3. Then he repeats the same data collection and distribution graph building procedure for the *second* segment of upvectors, and so on until he has reached and completed the maximum number of segments found for upvectors in the historical period under study (I have found nine segments to be maximum, but it could be larger or smaller in some periods).

He repeats the same data collection/distribution graph exercise for high to close changes, just as with the random walk model, for the first segments of all upvectors in the historical period under study, the second segment, and so on through the highest (maximum) segment found in an upvector. He does this also for the close to low price changes and the (open-low)/(high-low) statistic to be able to calculate open prices per the random walk model.

Finally, this whole set of procedures is repeated for the down vectors, cases 1 through 3 in Figure 4–6.

Whew! Good thing we have computers!

Constructing Price Vectors

Once the data has been collected and properly grouped and averages calculated for each cell (Figure 4–6, case 3), the task of creating prices is relatively straightforward (but we are still grateful to computers!).

The price construction procedures are as follows (refer to Figure 4–7):

1. *Alternate constructing upvectors and downvectors.* Start with (randomly) an upvector or downvector—I usually give each a 50 percent chance, since there are virtually the same number of each in any longer, real period. (Pictorially, case 1). Then alternate between upvector and downvector construction from that point on.

2. *Determine vector segment length.* Randomly choose from the vector segment distribution graph (Figure 4–6, case 1) the

FIGURE 4-7

Simple Price Vector Model—Data Generation

1. Start as Upvector or Downvector

2. Randomly Choose Vector Length (no. of segments)

3. Randomly Create O, H, L, C for Each Vector Segment

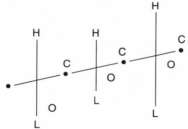

Segment = Period of time (e.g., day/week/month)

length or number of price changes that that up- or down-vector will contain.

3. *Create prices for each segment of the vector.* For each price vector segment so determined in 2 above, create close to close, open, high, and low prices from the price change graphs constructed in Figure 4–6 case 3, for the appropriate type of price and segment (price change) number in that price vector.

For example, use the second leftmost distribution graph, top line of case 3, for an upvector to randomly choose a cell value for the close to close price change for the second piece or segment of an upvector. Using the random walk formula, he will then define the closing price for that second close of the upvector being created, as the prior close plus the close-to-close change he found by randomly selecting from the close-to-close change distribution graph referred to before. Next, after completing construction of the current price vector, he should go back to (1), until all the new period's prices have been constructed.

EXAMPLES OF PRICE MODELS

The following tables and charts give tabular and graphical representations of all three models for a futures and a stock, for two different time periods.

Chart 4–5 shows Japanese yen futures' continous contract prices for most of 1995. The period was marked by two strong trends, one up and one down.

Table 4–1 lists the high, low, close, and open fraction changes in the random walk model formulas to create prices. The first column lists 20 cells' average values for the open fraction change (where the open price is in relation to the high–low range). The first value, 1.0, tells us if the random number generator produced a number 0.97 (or anywhere between 0.95 and 1.0) it would pick that cell and we would apply its number (1.0) to the high–low range and assign the top of the range (the high price itself) as the open price value. Other cell choices would allow the open to be placed somewhere between the high and low prices. For example, the 16th cell has a value of 0.2059, so the open price would be assigned a value of 20.59 percent of the range, about one-fifth of the way from low to high price.

Similarly, the last column shows 20 cell values (rows) of close to close values ranging from +.0259 to −.0143. If the computer picked the top cell, it would assign a closing price today of +.0259 points for the yen above yesterday's closing price. The third column over, C-L, tells us the computer will subtract the chosen cell value from today's close price to arrive at a low price value for today: If it chose the 11th cell, it would subtract .0040 points off today's calculated close (we just did that) to arrive at a low price value. To get the high price for today we add the value of a chosen cell (randomly, by the computer) in column 2 (H-C) to the already determined close price to get today's high price. Then we go through the choice of high-low fraction cell value, column 1, to get the proper fraction to multiply by the high-low range (we just determined the high and low prices) and obtain the open price value, as per previous discussion. The

CHART 4-5

Japanese Yen—Continuous Contract (01/01/95–10/06/95)

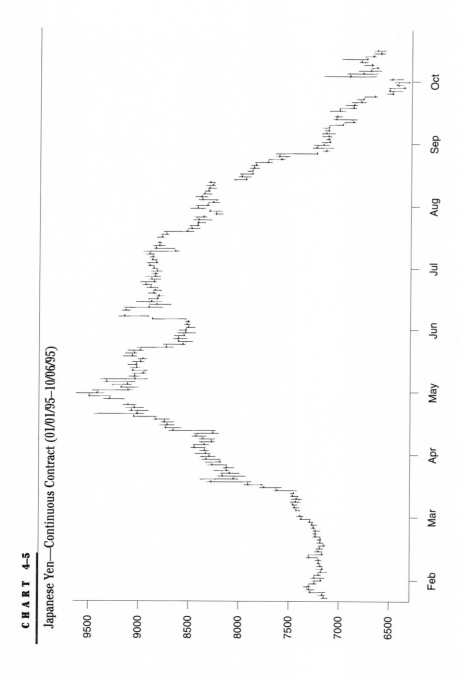

TABLE 4-1

Random Walk Model, Price Change Values; 20 Cells (Values)
Japanese Yen—Continuous Contract (01/01/95–10/06/95)

(O-L)/(H-L)	H-C	C-L	C-C
+1.0000	+0.0316	+0.0292	+0.0259
+0.9773	+0.0164	+0.0167	+0.0140
+0.9501	+0.0130	+0.0140	+0.0090
+0.9062	+0.0107	+0.0113	+0.0060
+0.8577	+0.0093	+0.0094	+0.0038
+0.8059	+0.0083	+0.0076	+0.0026
+0.7380	+0.0073	+0.0063	+0.0014
+0.6773	+0.0063	+0.0055	+0.0005
+0.6132	+0.0056	+0.0048	-0.0002
+0.5441	+0.0050	+0.0045	-0.0011
+0.4944	+0.0045	+0.0040	-0.0017
+0.4442	+0.0040	+0.0033	-0.0024
+0.3457	+0.0036	+0.0028	-0.0030
+0.2829	+0.0033	+0.0025	-0.0038
+0.2491	+0.0031	+0.0021	-0.0052
+0.2059	+0.0027	+0.0018	-0.0066
+0.1417	+0.0021	+0.0016	-0.0075
+0.0919	+0.0018	+0.0012	-0.0087
+0.0517	+0.0015	+0.0009	-0.0105
+0.0151	+0.0009	+0.0005	-0.0143

open price is the last one to be calculated but shows up in the table as the first set values of (column 1).

These numbers were generated for 20 cells. The number of cells was our choice: More cells mean more choices for the computer and more price combinations, but the number/average in each is less accurate. We can retain more cells if we increase the size of the period to still get good cell accuracy and more combinations, to look and feel more like real data. But in doing so we may be representing a bigger and more-mixed price period than we wanted. Good period choice is so important!

Charts 4–6 and 4–7 graph the values for the four statistics. Chart 4–6 shows the open fraction change for each of 20 cells. Chart 4–7 does the same for the other three statistics: close to close change; high to close change; and close to low price change.

Table 4–2 does the same thing Table 4–1 does except that there are 50 cells, not 20. Note that there is a wider spread of values (especially for close to close changes, column 4) and a finer gradation (less change/difference) from cell to cell.

CHART 4-6

Japanese Yen—Continuous Contract (01/01/95–10/06/95)
Random Walk Model, (Open-Low)/(High-Low), 20 Cell Values

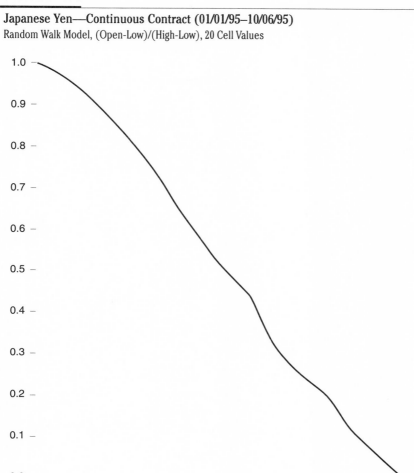

Table 4–3 gives information about change cells also, but for a different model, the sequential walk. Some of the statistics are similar, such as the H-O, or high to open change, instead of the H-C change for the random walk model, and the numbers are not far apart. But the major difference is the O-C statistic (first column) versus the C-C statistic for the random walk. The numbers are generally smaller—the top one for the O-C

CHART 4–7

Japanese Yen—Continuous Contract (01/01/95–10/06/95)
Random Walk Model, (20 Cells)

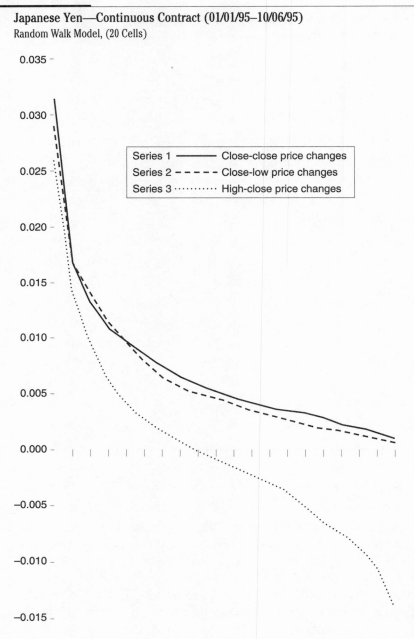

TABLE 4–2

Random Walk Model, Price Change Values; 50 Cells (Values)
Japanese Yen—Continuous Contract (01/01/95–10/06/95)

(O-L)/(H-L)	H-C	C-L	C-C
+1.0000	+0.0382	+0.0385	+0.0361
+1.0000	+0.0287	+0.0237	+0.0210
+0.9933	+0.0203	+0.0192	+0.0180
+0.9772	+0.0160	+0.0167	+0.0152
+0.9679	+0.0146	+0.0152	+0.0128
+0.9574	+0.0133	+0.0144	+0.0104
+0.9425	+0.0127	+0.0136	+0.0095
+0.9257	+0.0116	+0.0126	+0.0082
+0.9049	+0.0104	+0.0113	+0.0066
+0.8815	+0.0099	+0.0100	+0.0059
+0.8654	+0.0095	+0.0096	+0.0050
+0.8431	+0.0090	+0.0090	+0.0043
+0.8191	+0.0086	+0.0082	+0.0039
+0.8015	+0.0081	+0.0072	+0.0035
+0.7696	+0.0077	+0.0066	+0.0031
+0.7393	+0.0073	+0.0063	+0.0024
+0.7177	+0.0070	+0.0060	+0.0020
+0.6918	+0.0064	+0.0056	+0.0017
+0.6612	+0.0061	+0.0054	+0.0014
+0.6404	+0.0059	+0.0051	+0.0010
+0.6072	+0.0056	+0.0047	+0.0008
+0.5862	+0.0053	+0.0046	+0.0004
+0.5542	+0.0051	+0.0045	-0.0000
+0.5199	+0.0048	+0.0043	-0.0002
+0.5055	+0.0046	+0.0041	-0.0004
+0.4891	+0.0045	+0.0039	-0.0008
+0.4729	+0.0043	+0.0037	-0.0010
+0.4587	+0.0040	+0.0033	-0.0014
+0.4042	+0.0039	+0.0031	-0.0015
+0.3654	+0.0037	+0.0029	-0.0018
+0.3259	+0.0035	+0.0027	-0.0022
+0.2987	+0.0034	+0.0026	-0.0024
+0.2798	+0.0033	+0.0024	-0.0029
+0.2673	+0.0032	+0.0023	-0.0032
+0.2577	+0.0031	+0.0022	-0.0040
+0.2340	+0.0030	+0.0020	-0.0047
+0.2238	+0.0029	+0.0019	-0.0052
+0.1989	+0.0026	+0.0018	-0.0058
+0.1743	+0.0023	+0.0017	-0.0061
+0.1399	+0.0022	+0.0015	-0.0063
+0.1204	+0.0020	+0.0015	-0.0070
+0.1051	+0.0019	+0.0013	-0.0074
+0.0789	+0.0018	+0.0010	-0.0079
+0.0639	+0.0017	+0.0010	-0.0084
+0.0505	+0.0014	+0.0009	-0.0097
+0.0360	+0.0012	+0.0007	-0.0111
+0.0206	+0.0009	+0.0005	-0.0127
+0.0025	+0.0008	+0.0004	-0.0146
+0.0000	+0.0004	+0.0003	-0.0199
+0.0000	+0.0002	+0.0002	-0.0291

TABLE 4-3

Sequential Walk Model, Price Change Values; 50 Cells (Values)

Japanese Yen—Continuous Contract (01/01/95–10/06/95)

O-C	H-O	O-L	(C-L)/(H-L)
+0.0132	+0.0434	+0.0360	+0.9880
+0.0073	+0.0240	+0.0284	+0.9562
+0.0053	+0.0207	+0.0208	+0.9288
+0.0043	+0.0186	+0.0167	+0.8966
+0.0034	+0.0167	+0.0154	+0.8737
+0.0024	+0.0144	+0.0137	+0.8548
+0.0020	+0.0132	+0.0123	+0.8377
+0.0017	+0.0121	+0.0113	+0.8095
+0.0014	+0.0108	+0.0110	+0.8013
+0.0012	+0.0102	+0.0106	+0.7896
+0.0012	+0.0096	+0.0101	+0.7718
+0.0010	+0.0089	+0.0093	+0.7584
+0.0009	+0.0081	+0.0090	+0.7439
+0.0008	+0.0077	+0.0085	+0.7269
+0.0006	+0.0073	+0.0080	+0.7076
+0.0005	+0.0069	+0.0076	+0.6824
+0.0004	+0.0066	+0.0073	+0.6590
+0.0004	+0.0063	+0.0066	+0.6412
+0.0003	+0.0061	+0.0062	+0.6085
+0.0003	+0.0059	+0.0060	+0.5695
+0.0002	+0.0054	+0.0058	+0.5337
+0.0001	+0.0050	+0.0055	+0.5130
+0.0000	+0.0047	+0.0052	+0.5011
+0.0000	+0.0046	+0.0049	+0.4818
-0.0001	+0.0043	+0.0045	+0.4475
-0.0001	+0.0041	+0.0042	+0.4299
-0.0001	+0.0038	+0.0040	+0.4066
-0.0002	+0.0037	+0.0038	+0.3895
-0.0002	+0.0035	+0.0035	+0.3617
-0.0002	+0.0033	+0.0034	+0.3391
-0.0003	+0.0030	+0.0030	+0.3212
-0.0003	+0.0028	+0.0028	+0.3040
-0.0005	+0.0027	+0.0026	+0.2935
-0.0006	+0.0026	+0.0023	+0.2811
-0.0007	+0.0023	+0.0022	+0.2612
-0.0008	+0.0021	+0.0019	+0.2400
-0.0009	+0.0020	+0.0017	+0.2195
-0.0009	+0.0018	+0.0015	+0.1993
-0.0010	+0.0016	+0.0013	+0.1908
-0.0011	+0.0015	+0.0011	+0.1801
-0.0012	+0.0010	+0.0010	+0.1639
-0.0013	+0.0010	+0.0008	+0.1363
-0.0015	+0.0007	+0.0007	+0.1295
-0.0018	+0.0005	+0.0006	+0.1163
-0.0024	+0.0004	+0.0005	+0.1051
-0.0029	+0.0003	+0.0003	+0.0896
-0.0034	+0.0002	+0.0001	+0.0732
-0.0040	+0.0001	+0.0000	+0.0475
-0.0061	+0.0000	+0.0000	+0.0274
-0.0086	+0.0000	+0.0000	+0.0143

column is +.0132 versus +.0361 for the random walk model (Table 4–2), and the lowest cell contains an average value of –.0086 for the O-C statistic of the sequential walk model, versus a larger negative value of –.0291 for the random walk model (Table 4–2).

Even more radical is the set of information presented in Table 4–4 for a simpler price vector model. As explained in the model description previously, the model includes information about the number of upmoves and downmoves, such as the maximum number of runs or segments encountered in an upmove or downmove; the number of cells needed to simulate the first segment or run of an upmove and a downmove; the number of runs or segments in each upmove and downmove encountered during the historical period used to collect representative price data; and finally, the open, high, low, and close price change cell values for each of the runs or segments of upmoves or downmoves that is exactly the same in appearance and use as the random walk model. Note that there are different values for the open, high, low, and close changes for each price segment for and within the upmove and downmove vectors.

If we shift to another market, stocks, we will find many similarities in the models. Chart 4–8 graphs Amdahl Corp. prices for 1990, another period of time. Prices behave in a choppy manner for much of the year except for a sharp downturn period in July and August when prices fell from the $18-per-share area to $11.

Table 4–5 and Charts 4–9 and 4–10 tabulate and graph the open, high, low, and close changes for the random walk model. The magnitudes are different than for the Japanese yen, of course, but the general curvature of the graphs is the same, as are the values in the tables relative to each other.

Table 4–6 has the same format, but slightly different statistics covered, for the sequential walk model, for Amdahl.

Finally, Table 4–7 presents simple price vector model statistics for Amdahl. The style and general number relationships are very similar to that for the Japanese yen: a maximum of approximately four segments for both; both upvector and downvector segment sizes seem to be exponentially distibuted (a large number of small runs or segments, a small number of large runs); and similar curvature in the open, high, low, and close change numbers from cell to cell and in each vector segment or run.

This tends to confirm similar market pricing mechanisms in different markets and times.

T A B L E   4–4

Simple Price Vector Model, Vector/Cell Information; Vector-Run Random Walk Price Distributions

Japanese Yen—Continuous Contract (01/01/95–10/06/95)

50	4	4	No. vector cells; Max. runs/vector uptrends; Max. runs/vector downtrends
33			No. cell in upvector run #1
13			run #2
4			run #3
2			run #4
50			No. cell in downvector run #1
14			run #2
7			run #3
4			run #4

Upvector runs (ranked)	Downvector runs (ranked)
4.00	6.00
3.00	6.00
3.00	3.00
3.00	3.00
3.00	3.00
3.00	3.00
3.00	3.00
3.00	3.00
2.00	3.00
2.00	3.00
2.00	3.00
2.00	3.00
2.00	3.00
2.00	3.00
2.00	2.00
2.00	2.00
2.00	2.00
2.00	2.00
2.00	2.00
2.00	2.00
2.00	2.00
2.00	2.00
2.00	2.00
2.00	2.00
1.00	2.00
1.00	1.00
1.00	1.00
1.00	1.00
1.00	1.00
1.00	1.00
1.00	1.00
1.00	1.00
1.00	1.00
1.00	1.00

(continues)

T A B L E   4–4 (continued)

Upvector runs (ranked)	Downvector runs (ranked)
1.00	1.00
1.00	1.00
1.00	1.00
1.00	1.00
1.00	1.00
1.00	1.00
1.00	1.00
1.00	1.00
1.00	1.00
1.00	1.00
1.00	1.00
1.00	1.00
1.00	1.00
1.00	1.00

O-C	H-O	O-L	(C-L)/(H-L)	
0.7766	0.0114	0.0301	+0.0279	
0.6400	0.0088	0.0217	+0.0193	
0.5721	0.0081	0.0190	+0.0169	
0.5194	0.0058	0.0177	+0.0159	
0.5118	0.0056	0.0167	+0.0142	
0.4980	0.0051	0.0151	+0.0107	
0.4870	0.0049	0.0146	+0.0104	
0.4083	0.0044	0.0141	+0.0098	
0.3756	0.0042	0.0122	+0.0092	
0.3178	0.0041	0.0115	+0.0085	
0.2787	0.0039	0.0104	+0.0068	
0.2685	0.0039	0.0099	+0.0066	
0.2606	0.0038	0.0092	+0.0064	
0.2555	0.0035	0.0091	+0.0060	
0.2305	0.0034	0.0084	+0.0055	
0.2208	0.0034	0.0073	+0.0053	Upvector run #1
0.2051	0.0033	0.0059	+0.0048	
0.2015	0.0032	0.0056	+0.0044	
0.1798	0.0031	0.0050	+0.0040	
0.1497	0.0030	0.0045	+0.0038	
0.1242	0.0028	0.0043	+0.0035	
0.1188	0.0025	0.0041	+0.0033	
0.0874	0.0023	0.0039	+0.0031	
0.0737	0.0021	0.0031	+0.0028	
0.0640	0.0019	0.0028	+0.0025	
0.0589	0.0019	0.0027	+0.0023	
0.0422	0.0017	0.0023	+0.0019	
0.0310	0.0013	0.0023	+0.0015	
0.0192	0.0012	0.0020	+0.0013	
0.0103	0.0009	0.0017	+0.0008	
0.0026	0.0007	0.0015	+0.0006	
0.0000	0.0004	0.0013	+0.0003	
0.0000	0.0001	0.0006	+0.0001	

(continues)

79

T A B L E 4–4 (continued)

O-C	H-O	O-L	(C-L)/(H-L)	
0.6178	0.0073	0.0281	+0.0247	
0.4754	0.0063	0.0166	+0.0163	
0.4639	0.0061	0.0153	+0.0127	
0.3123	0.0048	0.0141	+0.0113	
0.2847	0.0041	0.0130	+0.0080	Upvector run #2
0.2473	0.0033	0.0099	+0.0058	
0.2007	0.0031	0.0058	+0.0037	
0.1482	0.0029	0.0047	+0.0027	
0.0990	0.0025	0.0044	+0.0018	
0.0528	0.0021	0.0023	+0.0015	
0.0274	0.0019	0.0016	+0.0010	
0.0000	0.0012	0.0013	+0.0009	
0.0000	0.0003	0.0007	+0.0006	
0.5205	0.0033	0.0180	+0.0182	
0.2835	0.0023	0.0084	+0.0074	Upvector run #3
0.0512	0.0010	0.0038	+0.0030	
0.0000	0.0006	0.0014	+0.0007	
0.4043	0.0035	0.0061	+0.0037	Upvector run #4
0.1759	0.0034	0.0027	+0.0022	
0.8234	0.0318	0.0094	-0.0043	
0.8234	0.0280	0.0075	-0.0043	
0.8234	0.0269	0.0070	-0.0043	
0.8193	0.0255	0.0063	-0.0046	
0.8140	0.0245	0.0058	-0.0047	
0.8053	0.0200	0.0053	-0.0048	
0.8011	0.0168	0.0051	-0.0049	
0.7997	0.0147	0.0050	-0.0049	Downvector run #1
0.7977	0.0131	0.0050	-0.0051	
0.7931	0.0127	0.0050	-0.0051	
0.7902	0.0125	0.0047	-0.0052	
0.7889	0.0119	0.0044	-0.0052	
0.7785	0.0118	0.0041	-0.0052	
0.7780	0.0115	0.0041	-0.0055	
0.7769	0.0109	0.0040	-0.0055	
0.7753	0.0104	0.0038	-0.0058	
0.7692	0.0103	0.0037	-0.0059	
0.7621	0.0094	0.0035	-0.0060	
0.7543	0.0087	0.0034	-0.0060	
0.7543	0.0083	0.0034	-0.0062	
0.7534	0.0081	0.0033	-0.0063	
0.7401	0.0081	0.0031	-0.0064	
0.7264	0.0080	0.0030	-0.0064	
0.7249	0.0079	0.0028	-0.0064	
0.7200	0.0079	0.0028	-0.0065	
0.7111	0.0075	0.0026	-0.0066	
0.6961	0.0074	0.0025	-0.0068	
0.6870	0.0073	0.0025	-0.0069	
0.6831	0.0073	0.0025	-0.0071	
0.6798	0.0070	0.0024	-0.0074	
0.6753	0.0069	0.0022	-0.0075	
0.6701	0.0065	0.0022	-0.0077	

(continues)

T A B L E   4–4 (concluded)

O-C	H-O	O-L	(C-L)/(H-L)	
0.6692	0.0062	0.0019	-0.0084	
0.6610	0.0061	0.0019	-0.0085	
0.6430	0.0060	0.0018	-0.0085	
0.6264	0.0058	0.0017	-0.0087	
0.6144	0.0058	0.0017	-0.0087	
0.6129	0.0054	0.0015	-0.0087	
0.6122	0.0049	0.0015	-0.0087	
0.6041	0.0046	0.0015	-0.0088	
0.5821	0.0046	0.0014	-0.0090	
0.5727	0.0041	0.0013	-0.0094	
0.5708	0.0041	0.0013	-0.0095	
0.5550	0.0040	0.0013	-0.0096	
0.5509	0.0040	0.0013	-0.0097	
0.5475	0.0040	0.0013	-0.0102	
0.5393	0.0035	0.0013	-0.0102	
0.5203	0.0034	0.0012	-0.0102	
0.5171	0.0031	0.0009	-0.0104	
0.5090	0.0031	0.0009	-0.0106	
0.7699	0.0144	0.0069	-0.0056	
0.7699	0.0104	0.0059	-0.0058	
0.7605	0.0084	0.0040	-0.0059	
0.7569	0.0084	0.0039	-0.0061	
0.7463	0.0082	0.0039	-0.0062	
0.7343	0.0078	0.0036	-0.0063	
0.7248	0.0076	0.0036	-0.0063	Downvector run #2
0.7022	0.0069	0.0034	-0.0064	
0.6893	0.0068	0.0031	-0.0068	
0.6878	0.0064	0.0031	-0.0073	
0.6876	0.0062	0.0029	-0.0075	
0.6756	0.0061	0.0028	-0.0075	
0.6659	0.0047	0.0022	-0.0076	
0.6419	0.0044	0.0022	-0.0081	
0.9678	0.0186	0.0090	-0.0012	
0.9275	0.0133	0.0068	-0.0014	
0.8440	0.0084	0.0055	-0.0018	
0.7306	0.0073	0.0039	-0.0068	Downvector run #3
0.5000	0.0063	0.0027	-0.0091	
0.2942	0.0025	0.0022	-0.0128	
0.1286	0.0001	0.0007	-0.0227	
0.6877	0.0099	0.0018	-0.0055	
0.6802	0.0087	0.0017	-0.0069	
0.6121	0.0073	0.0016	-0.0078	Downvector run #4
0.4056	0.0062	0.0015	-0.0083	

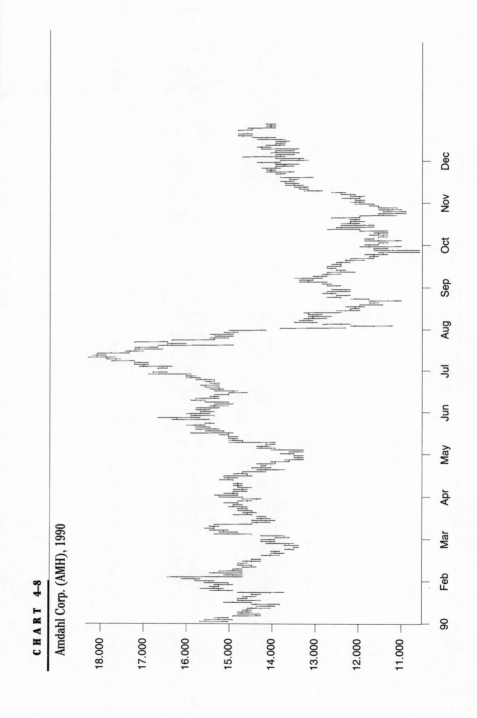

CHART 4-8

Amdahl Corp. (AMH), 1990

TABLE 4–5

Random Walk Model, Price Change Values; 50 Cells (Values)

Amdahl Corp. (AMH), 1990

(O-L)/(H-L)	H-C	C-L	C-C
+1.0000	+1.1750	+1.2250	+0.8044
+1.0000	+0.8750	+0.9000	+0.6794
+1.0000	+0.6750	+0.7500	+0.5856
+1.0000	+0.6250	+0.6250	+0.4919
+1.0000	+0.5500	+0.6250	+0.4919
+1.0000	+0.5000	+0.6250	+0.3981
+1.0000	+0.5000	+0.6250	+0.3356
+1.0000	+0.5000	+0.5500	+0.2419
+1.0000	+0.3750	+0.5000	+0.2419
+1.0000	+0.3750	+0.5000	+0.2419
+1.0000	+0.3750	+0.4750	+0.2419
+1.0000	+0.3750	+0.3750	+0.1794
+0.9653	+0.3750	+0.3750	+0.1169
+0.8667	+0.3750	+0.3750	+0.1169
+0.8000	+0.3500	+0.3750	+0.1169
+0.7856	+0.2500	+0.3750	+0.1169
+0.7500	+0.2500	+0.3750	+0.1169
+0.7500	+0.2500	+0.3750	+0.1169
+0.7095	+0.2500	+0.3750	-0.0081
+0.6667	+0.2500	+0.3500	-0.0081
+0.6667	+0.2500	+0.2500	-0.0081
+0.6667	+0.2500	+0.2500	-0.0081
+0.6533	+0.2500	+0.2500	-0.0081
+0.5711	+0.2500	+0.2500	-0.0081
+0.5000	+0.2500	+0.2500	-0.0081
+0.5000	+0.2500	+0.2500	-0.0706
+0.5000	+0.1250	+0.2500	-0.1331
+0.5000	+0.1250	+0.2500	-0.1331
+0.5000	+0.1250	+0.2250	-0.1331
+0.4089	+0.1250	+0.1250	-0.1331
+0.3333	+0.1250	+0.1250	-0.1331
+0.3333	+0.1250	+0.1250	-0.1331
+0.3333	+0.1250	+0.1250	-0.1331
+0.3333	+0.1250	+0.1250	-0.1331
+0.2767	+0.1250	+0.1250	-0.1644
+0.2500	+0.1250	+0.1250	-0.2581
+0.2300	+0.1250	+0.1250	-0.2581
+0.2000	+0.1000	+0.1250	-0.2581
+0.1667	+0.0000	+0.1250	-0.2581
+0.1321	+0.0000	+0.1250	-0.2581
+0.0222	+0.0000	+0.0750	-0.2581
+0.0000	+0.0000	+0.0000	-0.2581
+0.0000	+0.0000	+0.0000	-0.2581
+0.0000	+0.0000	+0.0000	-0.3831
+0.0000	+0.0000	+0.0000	-0.3831
+0.0000	+0.0000	+0.0000	-0.3831
+0.0000	+0.0000	+0.0000	-0.3831
+0.0000	+0.0000	+0.0000	-0.3831
+0.0000	+0.0000	+0.0000	-0.3831
+0.0000	+0.0000	+0.0000	-0.3831

CHART 4–9

Amdahl Corp. (AMH), 1990

Random Walk Model, (Open-Low)/(High-Low), 50 Cell Values

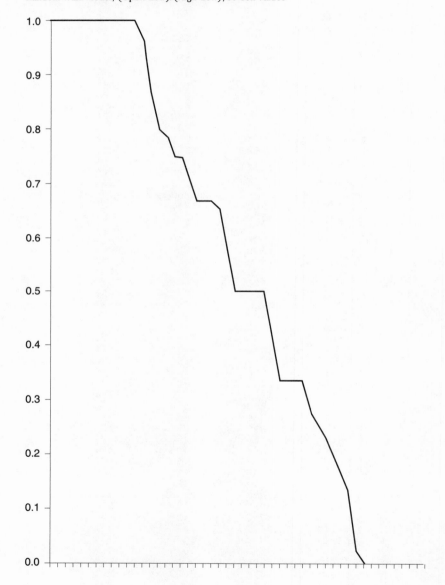

C H A R T   4–10

Amdahl Corp. (AMH), 1990
Random Walk Model (50 cells)

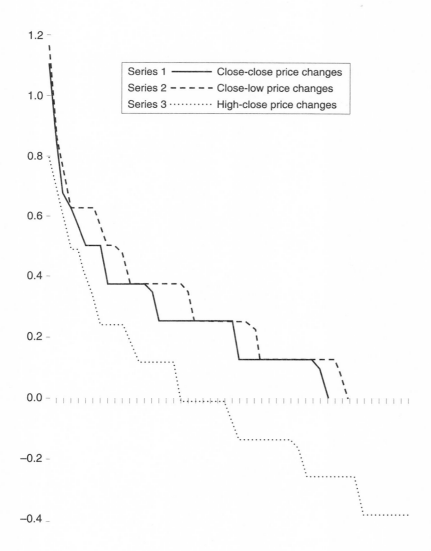

TABLE 4–6

Sequential Walk Model, Price Change Values; 50 Cells (Values)
Amdahl Corp. (AMH), 1990

C-C	H-O	O-L	(C-L)/(H-L)
+0.6231	+1.0313	+1.6256	+1.0021
+0.3731	+0.9063	+1.0319	+1.0021
+0.3106	+0.8750	+0.8756	+1.0021
+0.2169	+0.7813	+0.8131	+1.0021
+0.1856	+0.7188	+0.7506	+1.0021
+0.1856	+0.6250	+0.6881	+1.0021
+0.1544	+0.6250	+0.6256	+1.0021
+0.0606	+0.6250	+0.6256	+1.0021
+0.0606	+0.5000	+0.5006	+1.0021
+0.0606	+0.5000	+0.5006	+1.0021
+0.0606	+0.5000	+0.5006	+1.0021
+0.0606	+0.5000	+0.5006	+1.0021
+0.0606	+0.3750	+0.5006	+1.0021
+0.0606	+0.3750	+0.3756	+1.0021
+0.0606	+0.3750	+0.3756	+1.0021
+0.0606	+0.3750	+0.3756	+0.8868
+0.0294	+0.3750	+0.3756	+0.8473
-0.0644	+0.3750	+0.3756	+0.8354
-0.0644	+0.3750	+0.3756	+0.8104
-0.0644	+0.2813	+0.3756	+0.7965
-0.0644	+0.2500	+0.3756	+0.7521
-0.0644	+0.2500	+0.2506	+0.7521
-0.0644	+0.2500	+0.2506	+0.7521
-0.0644	+0.2500	+0.2506	+0.7521
-0.0644	+0.2500	+0.2506	+0.7009
-0.0644	+0.2500	+0.2506	+0.6688
-0.0644	+0.2500	+0.2506	+0.6688
-0.0644	+0.2500	+0.2506	+0.6688
-0.0644	+0.2500	+0.2506	+0.6313
-0.0644	+0.2188	+0.2506	+0.5949
-0.0644	+0.1250	+0.2506	+0.5021
-0.0644	+0.1250	+0.2506	+0.5021
-0.0644	+0.1250	+0.2506	+0.5021
-0.0644	+0.1250	+0.1256	+0.5021
-0.0644	+0.1250	+0.1256	+0.5021
-0.0644	+0.1250	+0.1256	+0.4842
-0.0644	+0.1250	+0.1256	+0.4021
-0.0644	+0.1250	+0.1256	+0.3792
-0.0644	+0.1250	+0.1256	+0.3354
-0.1269	+0.1250	+0.1256	+0.3354
-0.1894	+0.1250	+0.1256	+0.3354
-0.1894	+0.1250	+0.1256	+0.3354
-0.1894	+0.1250	+0.1256	+0.3354
-0.1894	+0.1250	+0.1256	+0.3354
-0.1894	+0.1250	+0.1256	+0.2975
-0.1894	+0.1250	+0.1256	+0.2521
-0.1894	+0.0625	+0.1256	+0.2521
-0.1894	+0.0000	+0.1256	+0.2168
-0.1894	+0.0000	+0.1256	+0.2021
-0.1894	+0.0000	+0.1256	+0.1771

TABLE 4–7

Simple Price Vector Model, Vector/Cell Information; Vector-Run Random Walk Price Distributions
Amdahl Corp. (AMH), 1990

20	4	5	No. vector cells; Max. runs/vector uptrends; Max. runs/vector downtrends
20			No. cell in upvector run #1
14			run #2
6			run #3
3			run #4
20			No. cell in downvector run #1
20			run #2
7			run #3
3			run #4
2			run #5

Upvector runs (ranked)	Downvector runs (ranked)
5.00	7.00
4.00	6.00
4.00	4.00
4.00	3.00
4.00	3.00
3.00	3.00
3.00	3.00
3.00	2.00
2.00	2.00
2.00	2.00
2.00	2.00
2.00	2.00
2.00	2.00
2.00	2.00
2.00	1.00
1.00	1.00
1.00	1.00
1.00	1.00
1.00	1.00
1.00	1.00

(O-L)/(H-L)	H-C	C-L	C-C	
0.8511	0.3723	0.7580	+0.7101	
0.6231	0.3191	0.7048	+0.6569	
0.4681	0.2128	0.6516	+0.6569	
0.3830	0.2128	0.6516	+0.5505	
0.2837	0.2128	0.5452	+0.5505	
0.2837	0.1596	0.5452	+0.4973	
0.2837	0.1064	0.5452	+0.4441	Upvector run #1
0.2128	0.1064	0.5452	+0.3378	
0.2128	0.1064	0.5452	+0.3378	
0.1702	0.1064	0.5452	+0.3378	
0.1560	0.1064	0.4920	+0.3378	
0.1418	0.1064	0.4388	+0.3378	

(continues)

T A B L E   4–7 (continued)

(O-L)/(H-L)	H-C	C-L	C-C	
0.1317	0.1064	0.4388	+0.2314	
0.1064	0.0000	0.3324	+0.2314	
0.0532	0.0000	0.3324	+0.2314	
0.0000	0.0000	0.3324	+0.1782	
0.0000	0.0000	0.3324	+0.1250	
0.0000	0.0000	0.2793	+0.1250	
0.0000	0.0000	0.2261	+0.1250	
0.0000	0.0000	0.1729	+0.1250	
0.5247	0.1944	0.4213	+0.5509	
0.2654	0.1944	0.4213	+0.4213	
0.2654	0.1296	0.4213	+0.4213	
0.2654	0.1296	0.4213	+0.4213	
0.2136	0.1296	0.4213	+0.3565	
0.1790	0.1296	0.4213	+0.3565	
0.1790	0.1296	0.3565	+0.2917	Upvector run #2
0.1790	0.1296	0.3565	+0.2917	
0.1790	0.1296	0.2917	+0.2917	
0.1617	0.0648	0.2917	+0.2917	
0.1358	0.0648	0.2917	+0.2917	
0.1358	0.0648	0.2917	+0.2269	
0.1358	0.0648	0.2917	+0.2269	
0.1099	0.0648	0.2917	+0.2269	
0.5833	0.2500	0.4375	+0.4375	
0.3333	0.1875	0.3750	+0.3125	
0.2917	0.1250	0.3750	+0.2500	Upvector run #3
0.1000	0.0625	0.3750	+0.2500	
0.0000	0.0000	0.2500	+0.1250	
0.0000	0.0000	0.1875	+0.1250	
0.2500	0.1875	0.4375	+0.5000	
0.1556	0.0625	0.3125	+0.1875	Upvector run #4
0.0000	0.0000	0.2500	+0.1250	
0.9007	0.8644	0.4787	-0.2340	
0.9007	0.7580	0.3191	-0.2340	
0.9007	0.7048	0.2128	-0.2340	
0.9007	0.5452	0.2128	-0.2340	
0.9007	0.4388	0.2128	-0.2340	
0.9007	0.4388	0.2128	-0.2340	
0.9007	0.4388	0.1064	-0.3404	
0.9007	0.4388	0.1064	-0.3404	
0.9007	0.3856	0.1064	-0.3404	
0.8475	0.3324	0.1064	-0.3404	Downvector run #1
0.7943	0.3324	0.1064	-0.3404	
0.7624	0.3324	0.1064	-0.3404	
0.7305	0.3324	0.1064	-0.3404	
0.6879	0.3324	0.1064	-0.4468	
0.6879	0.2261	0.1064	-0.4468	
0.6170	0.2261	0.0000	-0.4468	
0.6170	0.2261	0.0000	-0.5000	
0.6170	0.2261	0.0000	-0.5532	
0.6170	0.2261	0.0000	-0.5532	
0.5414	0.2261	0.0000	-0.5532	

(continues)

T A B L E   4–7 (concluded)

(O-L)/(H-L)	H-C	C-L	C-C	
0.8681	0.5313	0.4167	-0.2500	
0.8681	0.5313	0.4167	-0.2500	
0.8681	0.4271	0.3125	-0.2500	
0.8681	0.4271	0.3125	-0.2500	
0.8681	0.3229	0.3125	-0.2500	
0.8681	0.3229	0.3125	-0.2500	
0.8681	0.3229	0.3125	-0.2500	
0.8681	0.3229	0.2083	-0.2500	
0.8681	0.3229	0.2083	-0.3542	
0.8681	0.3229	0.2083	-0.3542	Downvector run #2
0.7014	0.2187	0.1042	-0.3542	
0.6597	0.2187	0.1042	-0.3542	
0.6597	0.2187	0.1042	-0.3542	
0.6597	0.2187	0.1042	-0.3542	
0.6597	0.2187	0.1042	-0.3542	
0.5903	0.2187	0.1042	-0.3542	
0.5903	0.2187	0.1042	-0.3542	
0.5347	0.1146	0.0000	-0.4583	
0.4514	0.1146	0.0000	-0.4583	
0.4514	0.1146	0.0000	-0.4583	
0.8265	0.4135	0.3462	-0.3077	
0.8265	0.3462	0.2115	-0.3077	
0.8265	0.3462	0.1442	-0.3077	
0.8265	0.3462	0.1442	-0.3750	Downvector run #3
0.8265	0.2788	0.1442	-0.3750	
0.8265	0.2788	0.0769	-0.3750	
0.7368	0.2788	0.0769	-0.4423	
0.7667	0.3500	0.1750	-0.2500	
0.6467	0.2750	0.1750	-0.2500	Downvector run #4
0.5267	0.2750	0.1000	-0.3250	
0.9132	0.4375	0.3750	-0.2500	Downvector run #5
0.4500	0.2500	0.0000	-0.5000	

GENERATION OF PRICE DATA

Once price data has been collected and transformed into the change distribution data discussed in the previous section, it is up to the researcher to properly construct price series. The following set of procedures discusses a general approach that will accomplish the construction. Many examples are then presented for different markets and models, and the data series generated are analyzed.

1. *Choose the historical period to emulate/represent the future.* As discussed previously, the choice of price period is all important, as we will see in some upcoming examples. Make sure the period not only represents your strong conviction about the (main)

type of period that lies ahead, but also choose other periods that could conceivably crop up. It is always prudent to include one of each of the main periods: trended up, trended down, and sideways. If possible, variations of these three basic markets should also be included: trend slightly up, moderately so, and strongly, for example.

2. *Choose price model(s) to represent price movements.* Price models explain and control how prices move. A random walk model plays down real cause and effect on prices and construes price changes as noncontrollable or random and unpredictable. The sequential walk model does the same but preserves the order of price changes in real-time trading; in other words, prices move from yesterday's close to open to high and low, then to today's close. The price vector model tracks strings of price changes as sustained bull or bear influences. See examples later for comparison of model price constructions.

3. *Collect price data and transform to price change distributions.* Per our discussion on data collection, gather the price data according to the statistics defined and needed for each distribution graph of the model chosen.

4. *Generate data (via computer) from the price change distibutions and appropriate formulas.* The computer will choose a random number between 0 and 1.0 and pick the corresponding cell value to add to the current price to arrive at the next new price for each price series created. For example, if the researcher had chosen a random walk model to use for the Japanese yen, chose the 01/01/95–10/06/95 period of continuous prices, and designated 20 cells for his price change distibutions for close to close changes, and so on (see Table 4–1), then a random value of 0.0192 generated by the computer would correspond to the fourth cell (0–.04999 being the 1st; .05–.09999 the second; .10–.14999 the 3rd; and .15–.1999 the 4th, and so on to the 20th at .95–.99999) and the new close price change value would be +.0060, which he would add to the last close price to get a new close price for the series. The computer starts off with an arbitrarily assigned price and ends with the designated number of prices—I suggest a minimum of a year period for each price

series for daily basis prices, and the same number of data points for other time bases (15-minute, hourly; more for tick-by-tick; perhaps less for monthly).

Examples of Generated Data

What do these generated price series look like? Do they really resemble true past prices, and could they give us different results and influence our choice of timing and portfolio methods? Are some models more accurate (thus better) than others? Could generated prices be more accurate for predicting method results than even past actual track records?

The following examples will help to shed some light and answer some of these vexing questions.

DIFFERENT MARKETS

The following price data/graphs and generated prices apply to one stock, Apple Computer. Three graphs (Charts 4–11, 4–12, and 4–13) display price action in sideways, uptrend, and downtrend markets, respectively.

Sideways Markets

Table 4–8 tabulates price change distribution data as 50 cells for Apple Computer for the period 5/06/91–12/20/91, a very much sideways period, when prices started and ended at about $50 per share.

Charts 4–14 through 4–23 give us a peek at just 10 year-long price scenarios generated by the computer using the distribution values and the random walk model in Table 4–8. We could just as easily have generated 100 or 1,000 or even 10,000 (each one takes a fraction of a second on a pentium computer, far less on a Cray). Each one starts at $50 per share, but the paths they take and the end result are often quite different. And, of course, this is what the trader/researcher desires: different, valid scenarios on which to test his timing methods.

The first one (Chart 4–14; see Table 4–9 for a printout of the whole generated price series) behaves something like the original series, pretty much bouncing between a little lower (46) to a little higher (64) than the start value (50). The moves are sharp, they do not last long, and prices generally scissor back and forth. The only criticism (we will get to model com-

Apple Computer (1992) Daily Prices in Sideways Market

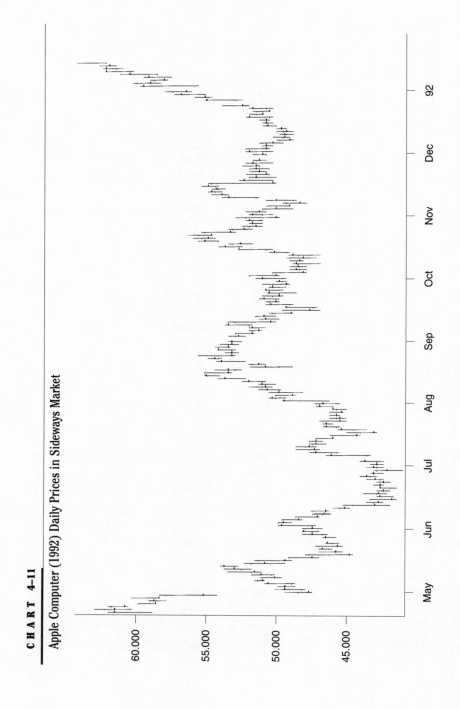

CHART 4-12

Apple Computer (October 1990–April 1991) Daily Prices in Uptrend

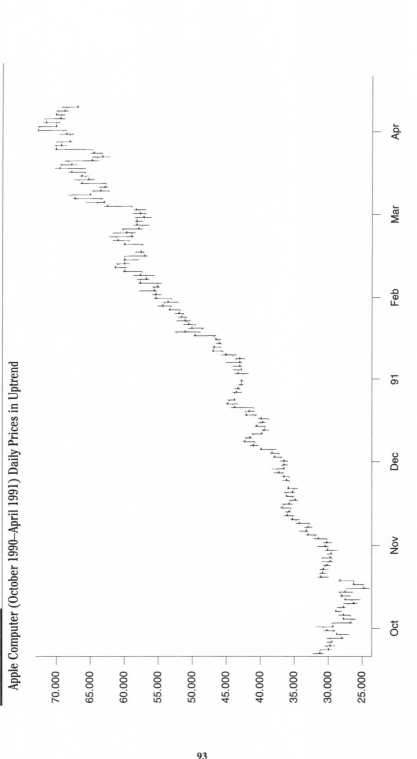

CHART 4-13

Apple Computer (January 1993–October 1993) Daily Prices in Downtrend

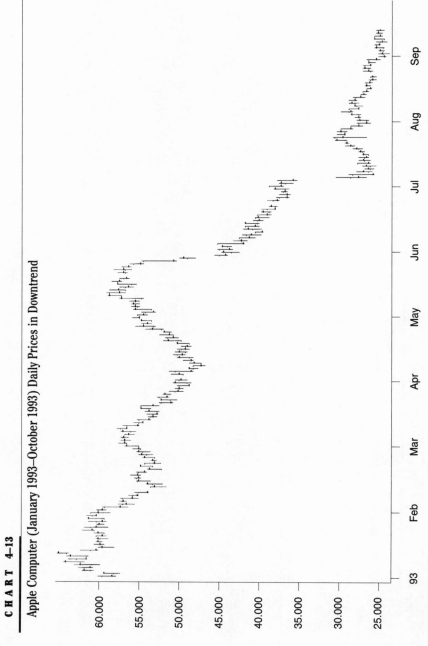

TABLE 4–8

Random Walk Model, Price Change Values; 50 Cells (Values)
Apple Computer (AAPL) Period: 5/06/91–12/20/91 (Sideways Market)

(O-L)/(H-L)	H-C	C-L	(C-C)
+1.0000	+3.7525	+2.9200	+2.8775
+1.0000	+2.6275	+2.3367	+2.4192
+1.0000	+2.2108	+2.0450	+2.0858
+1.0000	+2.0025	+1.8783	+1.5858
+1.0000	+1.9192	+1.7533	+1.5025
+1.0000	+1.7525	+1.7533	+1.1692
+1.0000	+1.6692	+1.6283	+1.0025
+0.9292	+1.5858	+1.5033	+0.8775
+0.8926	+1.5025	+1.4617	+0.8358
+0.8796	+1.2942	+1.2533	+0.8358
+0.8571	+1.2525	+1.2533	+0.8358
+0.8413	+1.2525	+1.2533	+0.7525
+0.8245	+1.2108	+1.1283	+0.7108
+0.8000	+1.1275	+1.0867	+0.5858
+0.8000	+1.0442	+1.0033	+0.5442
+0.7804	+1.0025	+1.0033	+0.4608
+0.7564	+1.0025	+1.0033	+0.3775
+0.7500	+1.0025	+1.0033	+0.3358
+0.7500	+0.9192	+1.0033	+0.3358
+0.7162	+0.8775	+0.9617	+0.2108
+0.6357	+0.8358	+0.8367	+0.1275
+0.6000	+0.7525	+0.7533	+0.0858
+0.6000	+0.7525	+0.7533	+0.0858
+0.5961	+0.7525	+0.7533	-0.0392
+0.5714	+0.7525	+0.7533	-0.0392
+0.5337	+0.7525	+0.6700	-0.1225
+0.5000	+0.6275	+0.6283	-0.1642
+0.5000	+0.5858	+0.6283	-0.1642
+0.5000	+0.5025	+0.5033	-0.1642
+0.5000	+0.5025	+0.5033	-0.2892
+0.5000	+0.5025	+0.5033	-0.3725
+0.4599	+0.5025	+0.5033	-0.4142
+0.4286	+0.5025	+0.5033	-0.4142
+0.4095	+0.5025	+0.5033	-0.4558
+0.4000	+0.5025	+0.5033	-0.5392
+0.4000	+0.5025	+0.5033	-0.6642
+0.3833	+0.4192	+0.5033	-0.6642
+0.3333	+0.3775	+0.5033	-0.6642
+0.3289	+0.3775	+0.4200	-0.7892
+0.2905	+0.3775	+0.3783	-0.9558
+0.2500	+0.3358	+0.3783	-1.0808
+0.2118	+0.2525	+0.2950	-1.1642
+0.2000	+0.2525	+0.2533	-1.1642
+0.2000	+0.2525	+0.2533	-1.2058
+0.1717	+0.2525	+0.2533	-1.2892
+0.1429	+0.2525	+0.2533	-1.4142
+0.1250	+0.2525	+0.2533	-1.4142
+0.1111	+0.2525	+0.2533	-1.5392
+0.0976	+0.2525	+0.2533	-1.6225
+0.0751	+0.1692	+0.2117	-1.9558

CHART 4-14

Random Walk Model—Generated Prices for Apple Computer (AAPL) from Actual Sideways Markets

Example #1

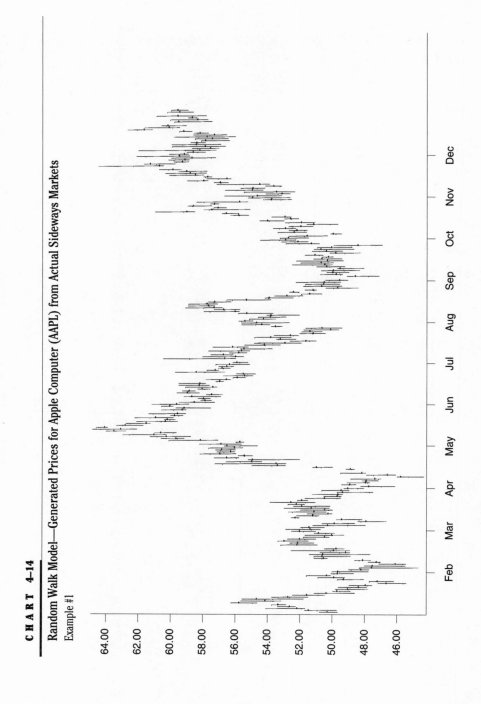

CHART 4–15

Random Walk Model—Generated Prices for Apple Computer (AAPL) from Actual Sideways Markets
Example #2

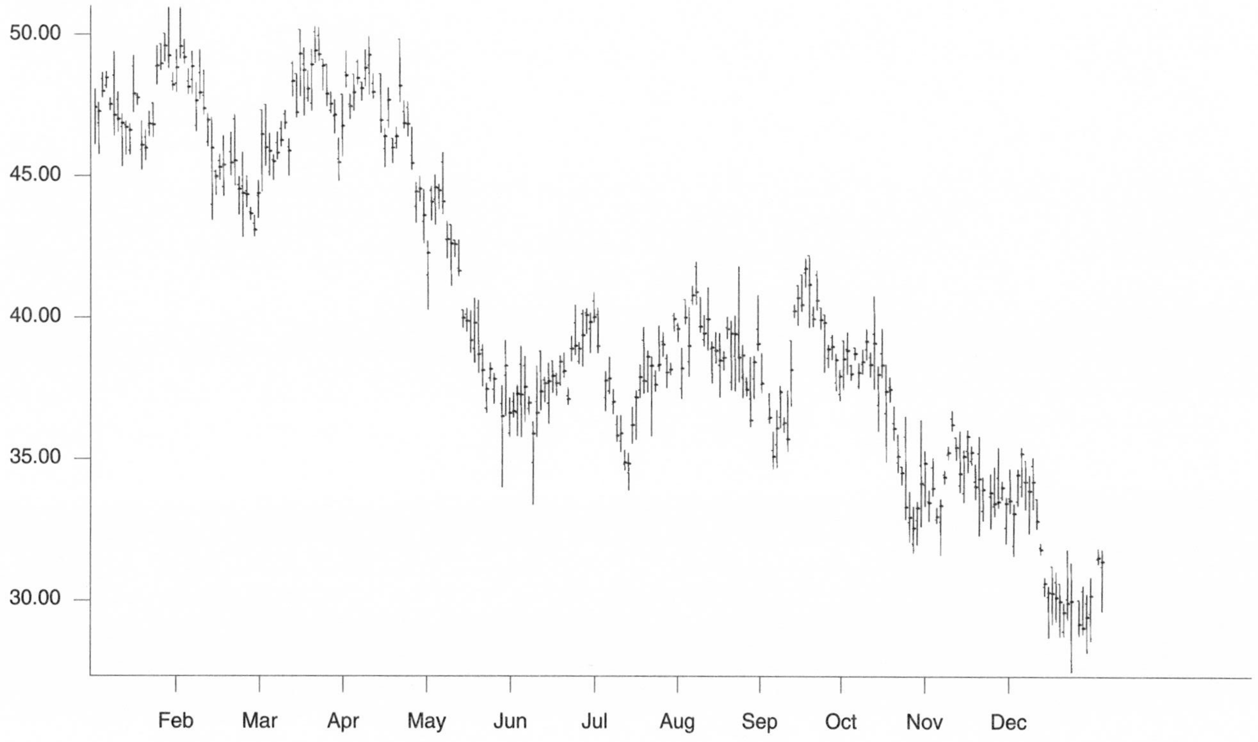

Random Walk Model—Generated Prices for Apple Computer (AAPL) from Actual Sideways Markets
Example #3

C H A R T   4–17

Random Walk Model—Generated Prices for Apple Computer (AAPL) from Actual Sideways Markets

Example #4

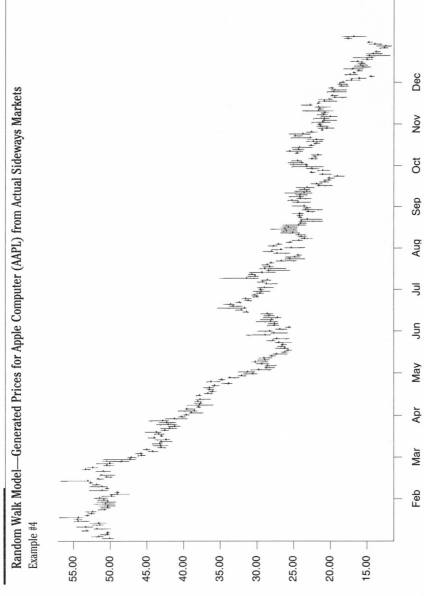

99

CHART 4-18

Random Walk Model—Generated Prices for Apple Computer (AAPL) from Actual Sideways Markets
Example #5

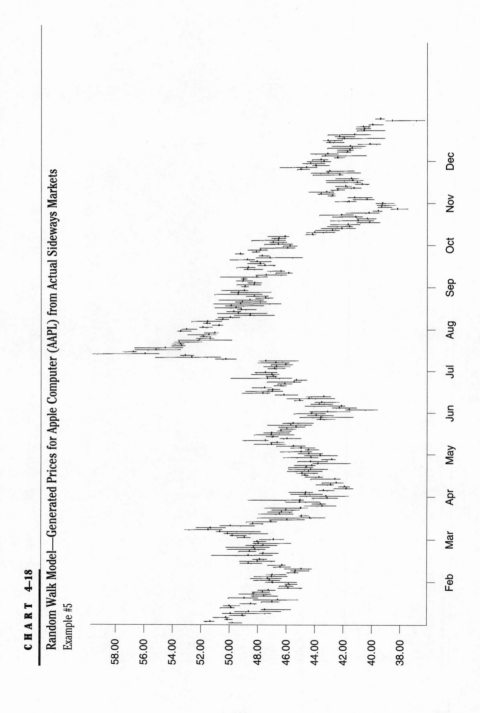

Random Walk Model—Generated Prices for Apple Computer (AAPL) from Actual Sideways Markets
Example #6

Random Walk Model—Generated Prices for Apple Computer (AAPL) from Actual Sideways Markets
Example #7

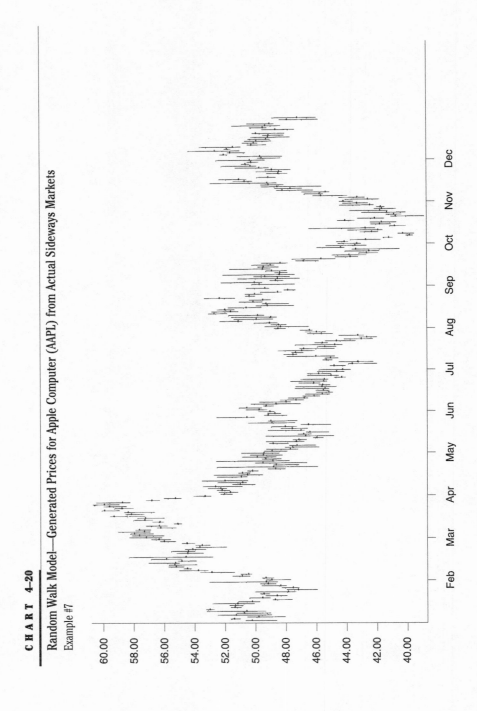

CHART 4-21

Random Walk Model—Generated Prices for Apple Computer (AAPL) from Actual Sideways Markets
Example #8

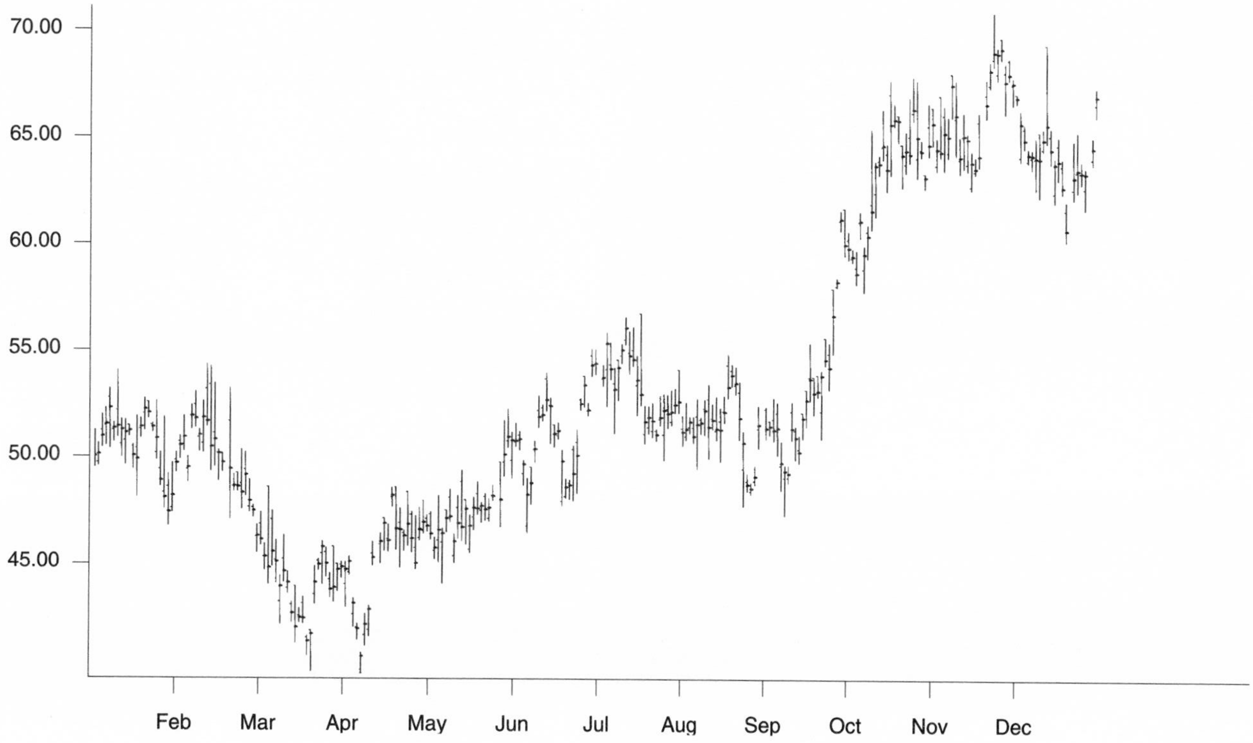

Random Walk Model—Generated Prices for Apple Computer (AAPL) from Actual Sideways Markets

Example #9

CHART 4-23

Random Walk Model—Generated Prices for Apple Computer (AAPL) from Actual Sideways Markets

Example #10

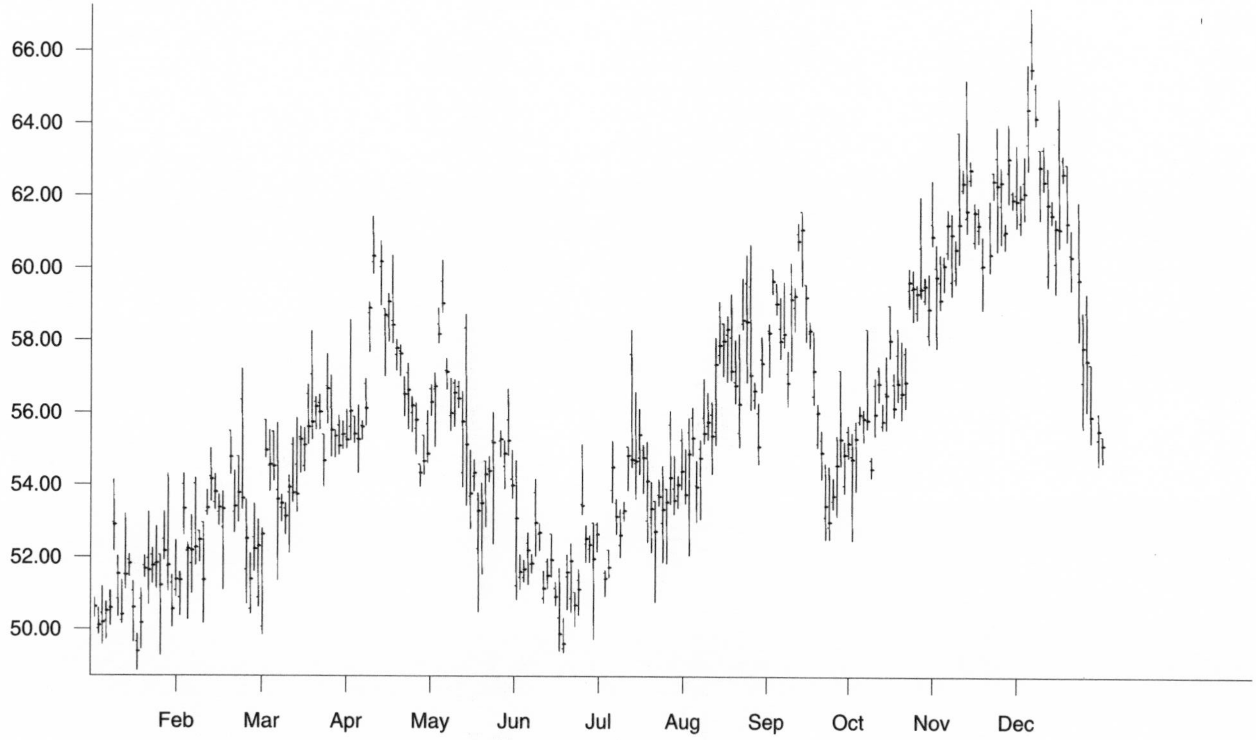

TABLE 4–9

Generated Prices for Apple Computer (AAPL) from Actual Sideways Market

Day	Open	High	Low	Close
1	50.05	50.502	49.372	50
2	50.62	51.422	49.416	51.169
3	51.613	53.799	51.377	51.88
4	52.415	53.094	51.963	52.341
5	53.429	53.429	52.549	53.052
6	54.623	55.974	54.343	55.471
7	53.347	55.352	52.846	53.849
8	53.372	55.27	51.473	54.393
9	52.312	53.44	51.184	52.437
10	50.546	52.151	50.145	51.273
11	50.55	50.819	48.314	50.067
12	49.22	49.656	48.566	49.403
13	48.69	49.492	47.486	48.739
14	48.575	49.327	47.572	48.075
15	47.526	48.664	47.241	47.661
16	45.314	46.875	45.119	46.372
17	47.418	47.418	45.913	46.916
18	49.38	49.38	47.749	49.002
19	50.59	50.59	48.918	49.588
20	51.302	51.302	49.796	50.049
21	49.566	49.763	48.382	49.385
22	49.228	49.723	47.468	49.346
23	48.506	48.685	47.429	47.932
24	48.02	48.02	44.348	47.268
25	45.375	47.732	45.184	47.229
26	45.331	46.818	45.145	45.815
27	46.805	47.486	46.731	46.984
28	48.037	48.323	47.317	47.82
29	50.33	50.825	49.986	50.239
30	50.827	50.827	48.572	50.325
31	50.585	51.122	47.366	50.286
32	49.232	50.458	48.619	48.872
33	49.815	52.251	48.621	49.624
34	50.062	50.213	48.957	49.46
35	52.881	52.881	50.626	51.879
36	52.236	52.343	50.837	51.84
37	53.054	53.054	51.173	52.676
38	51.39	52.472	50.717	51.72
39	51.475	51.475	49.886	50.181
40	49.676	51.394	48.972	49.725
41	50.096	50.813	49.558	50.561
42	51.48	52.233	50.727	51.73
43	50.971	52.568	50.438	51.066
44	51.551	51.655	50.19	51.152
45	48.736	50.907	47.651	49.988
46	48.722	50.326	48.321	49.574
47	47.932	48.121	46.365	47.618
48	48.045	49.457	47.868	49.121
49	51.818	52.252	51.746	51.999
50	50.713	51.921	50.54	50.918

(continues)

T A B L E   4–9 (continued)

Day	Open	High	Low	Close
51	50.879	51.256	49.709	49.962
52	52.174	52.425	50.086	50.839
53	49.923	51.678	49.672	50.175
54	51.981	52.68	49.883	51.011
55	50.746	52.1	49.844	51.597
56	52.436	52.436	51.43	51.933
57	51.358	53.563	50.766	52.269
58	51.858	51.858	51.227	51.605
59	49.404	51.402	49.188	50.191
60	49.231	50.238	49.149	49.402
61	49.337	50.949	49.068	49.363
62	47.412	49.41	47.196	49.074
63	50.371	50.371	48.657	49.16
64	48.137	48.999	47.784	48.746
65	46.681	47.959	45.829	47.457
66	48.688	49.129	48.248	48.626
67	47.521	48.798	47.417	47.67
68	47.598	47.883	46.878	47.631
69	46.855	48.595	46.714	47.092
70	44.97	45.722	43.967	45.47
71	47.162	47.6	45.803	46.306
72	49.186	49.186	47.639	47.892
73	48.497	48.855	48.35	48.603
74	50.404	50.942	49.686	50.689
75	53.441	54.694	52.605	53.108
76	56.476	56.947	52.566	53.194
77	55.397	56.283	54.069	54.697
78	53.007	54.91	51.738	54.658
79	55.638	56.997	55.491	56.244
80	55.13	55.54	54.66	55.163
81	57.248	57.876	55.662	56.665
82	56.401	56.837	55.748	56.001
83	56.618	56.922	55.708	56.545
84	57.342	57.342	55.253	55.756
85	55.431	56.386	54.339	56.217
86	57.252	57.889	55.342	56.595
87	55.612	55.684	55.178	55.431
88	59.769	59.769	56.763	57.85
89	59.263	60.272	58.85	59.353
90	60.502	60.942	58.436	59.939
91	62.187	62.611	59.939	60.692
92	59.507	60.656	59.316	60.278
93	63.031	63.658	62.403	63.156
94	64.011	64.495	61.739	62.742
95	64.091	64.248	63.533	63.745
96	62.614	63.042	61.328	62.456
97	62.156	62.42	60.914	61.167
98	60.252	61.755	59.25	60.003
99	59.713	60.049	59.377	59.88
100	60.933	61.885	59.504	60.591
101	59.176	59.679	58.924	59.427

(continues)

TABLE 4–9 (continued)

Day	Open	High	Low	Close
102	60.744	61.016	58.76	59.263
103	59.474	60.227	58.721	58.974
104	58.886	59.354	57.224	58.852
105	60.232	60.232	59.476	59.729
106	59.69	60.818	58.562	59.315
107	57.524	59.153	56.981	58.234
108	57.568	57.823	57.192	57.57
109	57.687	57.992	57.236	57.656
110	56.896	58.87	56.614	58.367
111	57.296	57.497	56.491	57.161
112	58.546	59.291	57.911	58.664
113	58.588	58.96	58.163	58.541
114	57.597	58.005	57.249	57.752
115	58.757	58.757	56.835	57.088
116	57.915	59.177	57.296	57.924
117	57.693	59.179	57.507	57.885
118	56.842	56.931	56.426	56.679
119	56.629	57.518	56.012	56.265
120	55.853	55.853	55.098	55.601
121	55.001	56.439	54.642	55.145
122	54.958	55.65	54.478	55.231
123	57.575	59.403	56.356	58.109
124	57.448	57.448	56.733	56.945
125	56.431	56.783	56.028	56.531
126	55.925	56.745	55.822	56.242
127	56.914	56.914	54.825	56.078
128	55.444	55.874	54.952	55.622
129	58.516	60.127	55.704	56.374
130	56.701	57.713	55.207	55.71
131	55.97	57.215	55.835	56.463
132	55.875	56.093	55.004	55.507
133	56.635	57.346	54.84	55.343
134	53.927	55.431	53.426	55.179
135	55.559	57.101	54.928	55.89
136	53.88	55.145	52.931	53.934
137	53.395	54.564	51.642	52.645
138	51.136	52.359	50.728	51.356
139	53.064	53.194	51.98	52.942
140	54.531	54.531	52.275	53.528
141	52.12	53.325	51.819	52.322
142	50.95	51.744	50.155	50.908
143	51.622	51.622	50.366	51.119
144	51.065	51.499	49.327	49.83
145	51.018	51.376	49.121	50.374
146	53.232	53.504	52.831	53.251
147	54.462	55.339	53.584	54.087
148	54.749	55.342	52.378	54.423
149	55.336	55.512	54.631	55.134
150	54.847	54.847	53.217	53.97
151	54.309	54.309	52.594	53.556
152	53.483	53.77	51.764	53.517

(continues)

T A B L E   4–9 (continued)

Day	Open	High	Low	Close
153	55.523	55.523	53.392	55.02
154	57.269	57.65	55.478	55.731
155	56.392	57.028	55.439	56.442
156	57.653	58.781	56.525	57.028
157	57.312	58.617	56.986	57.364
158	58.578	58.578	56.822	57.45
159	57.027	57.372	55.991	56.994
160	55.896	56.29	53.535	55.038
161	53.666	53.877	52.121	53.624
162	51.791	53.296	51.54	52.543
163	51.631	51.631	50.376	51.129
164	51.832	52.384	51.753	52.131
165	50.856	51.428	50.713	50.925
166	49.637	50.138	48.133	49.386
167	49.314	51.515	49.135	50.388
168	51.393	51.393	49.262	50.265
169	49.567	51.978	49.223	50.226
170	49.928	50.147	48.767	49.27
171	47.498	48.817	46.852	48.314
172	49.209	50.485	49.105	49.483
173	49.283	50.072	48.691	49.694
174	49.002	50.408	48.027	49.655
175	49.052	49.41	47.779	49.241
176	49.886	50.705	48.949	50.077
177	50.955	52.207	49.702	50.205
178	51.669	51.669	49.663	50.416
179	50.002	51.963	49.041	50.044
180	50.005	50.882	49.127	50.38
181	50.099	50.385	49.671	49.966
182	50.539	51.43	50.299	50.802
183	48.95	49.89	48.01	49.513
184	50.507	50.977	49.096	50.099
185	50.238	50.854	48.39	50.435
186	50.649	50.649	48.518	49.771
187	48.557	49.652	46.646	48.149
188	51.777	52.613	50.524	51.027
189	52.05	52.866	51.235	51.863
190	53.006	54.202	51.988	52.616
191	52.955	52.955	51.199	52.452
192	51.464	52.416	50.035	51.288
193	49.499	49.835	49.163	49.666
194	53.088	53.088	51.332	52.085
195	51.454	52.423	51.293	51.921
196	52.993	53.385	52.004	52.632
197	52.19	52.429	50.923	51.676
198	49.865	51.306	49.384	50.887
199	52.42	52.642	50.802	51.639
200	53.62	54.228	52.722	53.725
201	52.248	52.688	51.808	52.311
202	52.526	53.483	52.269	52.647
203	55.462	56.027	54.897	55.525

(continues)

T A B L E 4–9 (concluded)

Day	Open	High	Low	Close
204	56.409	56.53	55.524	56.277
205	58.897	60.615	58.193	58.696
206	57.317	57.659	54.82	57.157
207	57.037	57.037	56.281	56.784
208	58.364	58.665	57.159	58.287
209	57.015	57.25	56.745	56.998
210	57.64	58.087	54.956	55.459
211	52.923	54.006	52.25	53.503
212	53.445	54.924	52.335	54.672
213	54.883	56.386	52.88	54.383
214	53.094	53.846	52.341	52.844
215	55.183	55.183	52.052	53.18
216	55.183	56.352	54.013	54.683
217	54.393	55.396	53.891	54.644
218	52.964	53.858	52.852	53.355
219	55.233	56.86	53.605	54.233
220	56.589	57.03	56.149	56.652
221	58.03	58.658	57.402	57.655
222	56.741	57.493	55.988	56.241
223	57.537	57.663	57.157	57.41
224	59.417	59.749	57.66	58.163
225	58.749	60.002	57.496	58.499
226	57.829	59.213	57.457	58.71
227	59.808	60.382	59.043	59.546
228	61.971	64.135	60.129	60.382
229	60.552	61.304	59.423	60.926
230	59.346	59.472	58.592	58.97
231	59.495	59.809	58.553	58.806
232	57.195	59.644	56.93	58.392
233	61.2	61.771	58.516	59.144
234	59.188	59.774	58.602	58.855
235	58.026	58.693	57.563	58.316
236	58.801	61.655	56.899	57.902
237	58.04	58.366	56.735	57.238
238	59.576	59.576	56.321	57.574
239	58.961	59.621	56.615	58.118
240	58.017	58.457	57.576	58.079
241	57.792	57.792	56.078	57.54
242	58.17	58.17	56.164	57.126
243	57.962	59.464	55.709	57.462
244	57.277	58.3	56.253	57.006
245	58.012	58.262	57.381	57.884
246	59.139	59.139	58.384	58.887
247	61.707	62.309	60.803	61.306
248	59.565	61.269	59.139	59.767
249	59.93	60.231	58.725	59.853
250	59.442	59.442	57.144	59.189
251	59.694	59.694	57.397	58.025
252	58.127	58.614	58.066	58.361
253	60.533	60.533	57.486	59.239
254	59.868	59.868	58.279	59.116
255	59.621	59.621	58.615	59.243

parison later) is that prices seem to reverse perhaps a little more than the real prices in Chart 4–11. Refer to Table 4–8 for the price change distributions.

Note that month dates have been affixed to the bottom of the chart: This is necessary to get the graphics program to plot, but the dates could have been any arbitrary ones.

A surprise is found in Chart 4–15 for another generated price series for Apple Computer. Prices whip around and reverse about the same as in Chart 4–14, but there is a decided drift/trend to the downside, and prices eventually fall to 30. This means, even randomly speaking, that there is a (good) chance of prices being trended (downward) in the future and this could be a shock and unpleasant surprise to the trader who counted on choppy/sideways markets!

Some of the other charts show surprises, too. Chart 4–17 shows a distinctly downward trend, from 50 to 15 and lower, something perhaps inconceivable if one strongly believed only narrow sideways markets (see Chart 4–11) could occur. A long position, or buying on dips, would have been disastrous. Chart 4–22 even shows two trends, one up and one down! Many do behave as the trader might have expected—prices chugging back and forth but not much over or under the start price.

Uptrend Markets

If we use another time frame (focusing on a strong uptrending period) for Apple Computer (see Chart 4–12 for actual prices for the period October 1990 to April 1991), choose the random walk model again, and gather and calculate price data for the change distributions, we will generate prices that look like the original series (ho-hum, no surprise) in Charts 4–24 and 4–25. The price change distribution values are shown in Table 4–10 and the price values are listed in Table 4–11 for the generated prices in Chart 4–24.

If we generated many price series (not just the two shown) we would probably get some charts with less drift or trend, and possibly some (rare) downtrends.

Downtrend Markets

This time we will concentrate on a downtrending period, from 1/14/93 to 10/01/93 for Apple Computer (see Chart 4–13 for graphical display of real prices), when prices collapsed from 65 to 25 in again a straightforward,

CHART 4–24

Random Walk Model—Generated Prices for Apple Computer (AAPL) from Actual Uptrend Markets
Example #1

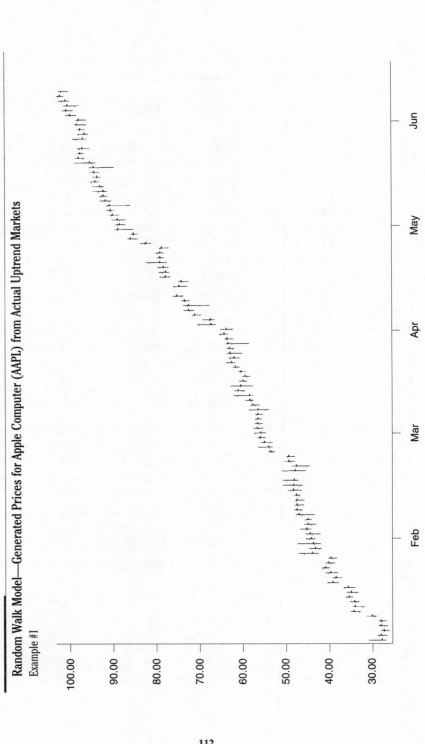

CHART 4-25

Random Walk Model—Generated Prices for Apple Computer (AAPL) from Actual Uptrend Markets
Example #2

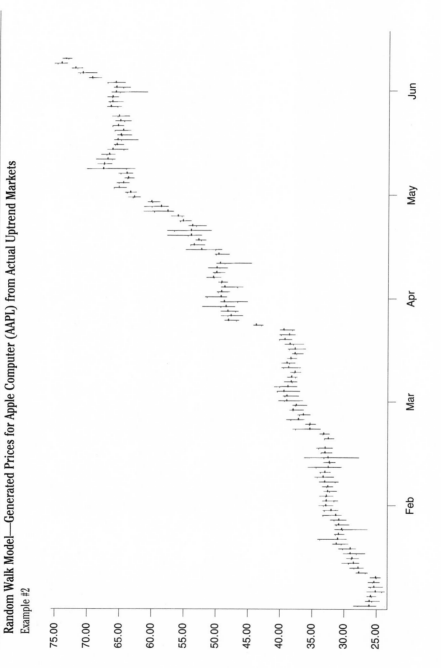

T A B L E 4–10

Random Walk Model, Price Change Values; 40 Cells (Values)
Apple Computer (AAPL) Period: 10/10/90–4/02/91 (Uptrend)

(O-L)/(H-L)	H-C	C-L	C-C
+1.0081	+3.7266	+4.8906	+4.3609
+1.0081	+3.1641	+4.0156	+3.6734
+0.9748	+2.6641	+3.6406	+2.6734
+0.9210	+2.4766	+3.1406	+2.1734
+0.9105	+2.1641	+2.8281	+1.7984
+0.9026	+2.1016	+2.5156	+1.6109
+0.8970	+1.8516	+2.3906	+1.4859
+0.8826	+1.6016	+2.1406	+1.2984
+0.8598	+1.5391	+2.1406	+1.1734
+0.8415	+1.3516	+1.8906	+0.9859
+0.8415	+1.3516	+1.8281	+0.9859
+0.8081	+1.3516	+1.6406	+0.8609
+0.7970	+1.3516	+1.6406	+0.7984
+0.7581	+1.2891	+1.6406	+0.7359
+0.7581	+1.1016	+1.6406	+0.7359
+0.7581	+1.1016	+1.6406	+0.6109
+0.7581	+1.1016	+1.5156	+0.4859
+0.7224	+1.1016	+1.4531	+0.4859
+0.6915	+0.9766	+1.3906	+0.4859
+0.6748	+0.9141	+1.3906	+0.2984
+0.6748	+0.8516	+1.3906	+0.2359
+0.6415	+0.8516	+1.3906	+0.1109
+0.6081	+0.8516	+1.2656	-0.0141
+0.5938	+0.8516	+1.2656	-0.0141
+0.5438	+0.7266	+1.2031	-0.0141
+0.4637	+0.7266	+1.1406	-0.0141
+0.4308	+0.7266	+1.1406	-0.0141
+0.4127	+0.6641	+1.1406	-0.0766
+0.4081	+0.6016	+1.1406	-0.1391
+0.4004	+0.6016	+1.0781	-0.2016
+0.3623	+0.6016	+0.8906	-0.2641
+0.2647	+0.6016	+0.8906	-0.2641
+0.2442	+0.6016	+0.8906	-0.3891
+0.2192	+0.6016	+0.8906	-0.5141
+0.2081	+0.6016	+0.8906	-0.5141
+0.1748	+0.6016	+0.8906	-0.5141
+0.1748	+0.6016	+0.8906	-0.5141
+0.1684	+0.6016	+0.8906	-0.6391
+0.1620	+0.5391	+0.8281	-0.7016
+0.1510	+0.4766	+0.7656	-0.7641

monotonous fall. If we again use the random walk model and gather price data and transform them into distributions found in Table 4–12, we can generate many such downtrends, two of which are shown in Charts 4–26 and 4–27. No surprise again—prices fall down in a steady stream, but some (real-looking) reactions to—rises in—the down market might catch the

TABLE 4–11

Generated Prices for Apple Computer (AAPL) from Actual Uptrend Markets

Day	Open	High	Low	Close
1	27.575	29.164	25.109	26
2	26.658	27.088	24.845	26.236
3	25.442	26.198	24.268	25.534
4	25.595	26.872	24.629	26.27
5	26.006	26.858	24.99	26.256
6	27.745	29.781	27.351	28.429
7	31.548	33.517	31.149	32.79
8	30.758	33.128	30.135	32.526
9	32.309	33.739	31.496	32.637
10	34.453	34.787	33.044	33.935
11	32.259	34.523	31.78	33.421
12	35.014	35.259	32.516	34.157
13	38.747	39.182	36.439	37.83
14	37.375	37.918	35.675	37.066
15	38.992	39.716	36.723	38.364
16	40.219	40.389	38.646	39.537
17	38.23	39.437	37.382	38.835
18	38.014	38.923	36.93	38.321
19	44.582	45.846	41.291	42.682
20	41.082	43.519	40.589	41.98
21	42.136	46.193	40.825	42.466
22	43.425	44.304	42.061	42.952
23	42.758	44.352	40.859	43.25
24	44.068	45.525	43.095	43.986
25	43.049	44.574	41.894	43.722
26	44.276	44.31	42.942	43.708
27	45.188	46.608	42.24	45.881
28	45.456	46.969	45.164	46.367
29	46.151	46.955	44.712	46.353
30	46.519	46.816	44.698	46.339
31	45.881	46.989	45.684	46.45
32	47.754	48.538	45.295	47.186
33	45.779	49.649	45.031	47.172
34	48.837	49.697	46.142	47.033
35	48.843	49.933	44.253	46.769
36	44.079	47.607	43.364	46.505
37	47.91	49.405	46.912	48.303
38	48.584	48.766	46.898	48.289
39	52.3	53.252	51.759	52.65
40	52.946	55.613	52.245	53.136
41	52.802	54.974	52.231	54.122
42	55.273	55.71	53.905	55.108
43	56.268	56.508	53.828	54.969
44	55.479	56.682	54.439	55.83
45	55.363	56.355	54.612	55.753
46	56.144	56.278	54.785	55.676
47	55.988	56.264	54.521	55.662
48	53.839	57.812	53.132	55.648
49	56.217	57.423	55.305	56.821
50	57.194	58.659	56.666	57.557

(continues)

115

T A B L E   4–11 (continued)

Day	Open	High	Low	Close
51,	60.509,	61.395,	56.777,	57.668
52,	59.219,	61.193,	58.7,	60.341
53,	59.759,	62.179,	56.874,	59.702
54,	58.591,	60.04,	58.297,	59.188
55,	58.179,	59.276,	57.408,	58.674
56,	59.695,	60.262,	58.519,	59.66
57,	60.954,	61.56,	60.067,	60.958
58,	62.663,	63.233,	61.178,	61.944
59,	62.344,	62.407,	59.914,	61.305
60,	62.063,	62.893,	59.463,	62.291
61,	61.66,	62.941,	61.324,	62.402
62,	61.878,	63.177,	57.809,	62.7
63,	63.056,	63.538,	61.545,	62.936
64,	64.458,	64.774,	62.781,	63.672
65,	61.969,	64.51,	61.517,	63.158
66,	69.61,	69.995,	65.69,	66.831
67,	67.149,	68.79401,	66.051,	66.942
68,	71.108,	71.092,	69.162,	70.61501
69,	71.801,	73.203,	70.83501,	72.10101
70,	72.396,	73.37601,	67.19601,	72.08701
71,	72.942,	73.675,	71.87,	73.07301
72,	73.806,	75.72301,	73.41801,	74.871
73,	75.453,	75.70901,	72.466,	74.357
74,	73.534,	74.44501,	72.202,	73.843
75,	77.855,	78.868,	76.375,	77.51601
76,	78.291,	79.041,	76.611,	77.50201
77,	78.73701,	79.34,	76.847,	77.98801
78,	81.25101,	82.013,	77.208,	78.84901
79,	78.756,	79.437,	77.944,	78.83501
80,	79.346,	79.798,	77.93,	78.82101
81,	78.72,	79.034,	76.791,	78.43201
82,	82.32001,	83.457,	80.964,	82.105
83,	84.456,	86.38,	83.95,	85.77801
84,	84.95801,	85.61501,	83.998,	85.076
85,	88.73901,	89.60101,	85.108,	88.749
86,	88.84701,	89.21201,	86.90701,	88.36
87,	88.29101,	90.19801,	87.01801,	88.846
88,	90.219,	90.746,	88.566,	90.019
89,	90.422,	91.357,	89.61401,	90.505
90,	91.387,	91.343,	85.85001,	90.741
91,	90.804,	93.01601,	90.33601,	91.72701
92,	92.78201,	92.94,	91.32201,	92.21301
93,	93.356,	94.676,	91.30801,	92.19901
94,	92.52,	94.84901,	92.106,	92.997
95,	94.956,	95.272,	93.27901,	94.17001
96,	93.72301,	94.758,	92.828,	93.65601
97,	94.27801,	95.244,	93.12601,	94.39201
98,	93.37601,	95.48,	89.61201,	94.50301
99,	94.83501,	99.091,	93.97301,	95.36401
100,	96.965,	98.76401,	96.58401,	98.037
101,	97.665,	98.25001,	96.757,	97.648

(continues)

T A B L E   4–11 (continued)

Day	Open	High	Low	Close
102,97.801,98.23601,95.493,97.134
103,98.719,99.534,96.16601,97.05701
104,98.038,98.02,95.77701,96.66801
105,97.772,98.256,96.51301,97.65401
106,96.55701,98.992,96.12401,98.51501
107,98.27,98.665,96.173,98.00101
108,99.95701,101.151,98.533,100.174
109,100.993,101.887,99.394,101.035
110,98.842,101.623,97.94301,100.771
111,102.048,102.859,100.366,101.257
112,102.954,103.282,101.664,102.555
113,102.305,102.893,100.463,102.291
114,101.887,102.379,96.886,101.777
115,102.977,103.24,100.997,101.888
116,102.798,102.976,100.983,101.874
117,100.575,102.837,99.844,101.735
118,104.493,105.385,102.642,103.533
119,103.505,105.246,102.878,104.519
120,105.875,106.419,102.989,105.817
121,105.421,109.092,104.1,105.928
122,105.723,110.141,102.773,106.414
123,108.117,110.939,107.571,110.087
124,109.983,110.175,108.307,109.573
125,110.18,111.973,108.043,109.309
126,114.549,114.522,111.154,113.67
127,112.822,114.758,110.515,113.656
128,113.214,114.494,111.689,113.142
129,114,117.855,112.987,114.128
130,115.45,116.653,114.41,115.301
131,118.435,120.389,118.021,119.662
132,118.729,120.25,116.007,119.148
133,123.278,123.673,121.18,122.821
134,124.524,124.971,121.166,122.807
135,124.514,124.895,121.652,123.543
136,124.246,124.631,121.888,123.529
137,122.929,124.367,122.624,123.765
138,126.568,128.353,123.798,124.626
139,127.374,127.776,124.908,126.424
140,127.28,127.262,125.019,125.91
141,127.512,127.498,125.755,126.896
142,126.781,129.421,125.928,128.069
143,132.14,134.282,131.539,132.43
144,132.067,134.268,131.275,133.416
145,138.5,139.191,134.261,137.089
146,137.073,137.427,135.684,136.575
147,136.32,136.725,134.17,135.811
148,138.033,138.586,136.593,137.984
149,142.956,143.197,141.142,142.345
150,140.542,142.683,138.69,141.831
151,142.469,145.294,141.676,142.817
152,145.174,145.467,142.974,144.115

(continues)

TABLE 4–11 (continued)

Day	Open	High	Low	Close
153	146.802	146.765	142.21	144.601
154	147.424	149.626	145.758	148.274
155	150.896	151.549	147.431	149.072
156	149.012	149.66	147.667	149.058
157	148.93	148.896	144.653	148.294
158	149.386	150.444	147.014	148.28
159	147.656	148.618	145.5	148.016
160	148.698	148.916	146.673	148.314
161	148.62	149.652	147.909	148.8
162	152.582	153.2	150.645	152.473
163	153.859	156.061	150.443	152.334
164	154.008	153.984	150.991	152.632
165	150.042	152.72	149.29	152.118
166	152.387	152.456	149.713	151.604
167	149.347	153.692	148.574	152.59
168	153.446	153.928	151.935	153.326
169	152.835	154.414	149.296	153.312
170	152.809	153.087	151.719	152.61
171	152.891	153.948	149.58	152.096
172	155.106	156.433	154.628	155.769
173	156	157.232	155.739	156.63
174	157.691	158.155	155.225	156.616
175	157.085	158.329	156.211	157.602
176	156.731	158.19	156.322	157.088
177	157.068	157.863	156.12	157.011
178	161.724	161.974	159.544	161.372
179	162.805	162.772	158.717	161.858
180	162.763	163.446	161.703	162.594
181	162.643	163.682	159.939	162.08
182	159.571	162.23	157.737	161.378
183	160.654	162.528	160.161	161.614
184	164.563	165.077	160.084	162.6
185	163.706	164.188	162.195	163.586
186	163.373	165.361	162.243	164.384
187	166.067	168.659	165.229	168.057
188	169.315	169.582	166.84	168.043
189	167.512	169.443	166.888	168.779
190	170.136	170.679	168.436	170.077
191	169.659	170.665	169.297	170.063
192	171.023	171.338	168.658	170.049
193	175.531	175.762	173.519	174.41
194	177.146	179.873	176.38	178.771
195	178.053	181.609	177.366	179.507
196	180.427	181.157	177.352	178.993
197	180.292	181.143	175.775	179.791
198	179.71	180.941	179.386	180.277
199	179.921	181.865	178.622	181.013
200	182.331	183.538	181.483	182.624
201	183.123	183.274	181.719	182.61
202	183.734	184.01	182.267	183.408
203	184.916	186.933	184.19	185.581

(continues)

118

T A B L E   4–11 (concluded)

Day	Open	High	Low	Close
204	185.288	186.794	184.801	186.067
205	187.012	187.155	185.35	186.553
206	187.36	187.453	183.773	186.164
207	187.889	187.877	186.384	187.15
208	186.136	186.863	184.245	186.386
209	187.227	189.536	185.231	186.372
210	186.264	188.022	185.029	187.17
211	187.222	188.133	185.89	186.781
212	188.266	189.056	186.626	187.517
213	189.055	190.105	187.425	188.253
214	188.558	189.903	187.66	188.551
215	186.744	188.389	186.396	187.787
216	189.713	190.124	187.194	188.585
217	186.997	189.673	186.43	188.071
218	190.116	190.096	187.603	189.244
219	190.022	190.832	188.839	190.23
220	191.063	191.255	188.825	189.716
221	187.552	190.741	186.936	189.452
222	188.837	190.04	187.797	189.438
223	190.639	191.776	189.283	190.424
224	189.811	192.262	189.019	191.41
225	192.839	193.373	190.005	190.896
226	191.459	193.234	191.116	192.382
227	199.99	200.47	195.102	196.743
228	201.22	202.08	198.525	199.416
229	200.439	202.004	198.011	200.152
230	200.311	201.552	198.497	200.638
231	200.596	201.163	199.42	200.561
232	200.663	200.649	198.906	199.797
233	198.75	201.135	198.267	200.408
234	201.326	201.808	199.815	201.206
235	200.966	201.606	199.301	200.942
236	204.284	204.592	201.599	202.74
237	201.43	203.453	199.898	202.726
238	201.604	202.751	198.008	202.024
239	200.501	203.424	199.681	201.322
240	201.629	202.41	200.417	201.308
241	200.925	201.271	199.091	200.544
242	199.414	201.007	199.077	200.28
243	200.819	202.18	200.437	201.578
244	203.216	203.478	201.61	202.876
245	203.589	204.214	202.471	203.362
246	203.227	204.575	202.207	203.848
247	203.261	205.06	202.88	203.771
248	204.618	204.984	203.179	204.257
249	205.872	206.845	203.852	204.993
250	204.783	205.456	203.276	204.729
251	204.813	206.692	202.574	204.215
252	204.797	205.303	202.81	204.701
253	205.521	206.039	204.359	205.437
254	209.853	210.275	208.532	209.798
255	208.231	211.136	207.643	209.784

T A B L E   4–12

Random Walk Model, Price Change Values; 60 Cells (Values)
Apple Computer (AAPL) Period: 1/14/93–10/4/93 (Downtrend Markets)

(O-L)/(H-L)	H-C	C-L	C-C
+1.0000	+3.4583	+2.7083	+1.8708
+1.0000	+2.6250	+2.0000	+1.6208
+1.0000	+1.8750	+1.9583	+1.4542
+1.0000	+1.6667	+1.7500	+1.2458
+1.0000	+1.5000	+1.6250	+1.2042
+1.0000	+1.5000	+1.5000	+1.1208
+1.0000	+1.5000	+1.5000	+1.0375
+1.0000	+1.3750	+1.5000	+0.9542
+0.9810	+1.2917	+1.5000	+0.8292
+0.9309	+1.2500	+1.4583	+0.7875
+0.8709	+1.2500	+1.3333	+0.7042
+0.8571	+1.2500	+1.2500	+0.5375
+0.8448	+1.2500	+1.2500	+0.4542
+0.8222	+1.2500	+1.2083	+0.4542
+0.8000	+1.1667	+1.1250	+0.4542
+0.7862	+1.1250	+1.0417	+0.4125
+0.7500	+1.0833	+1.0000	+0.3292
+0.7500	+1.0000	+1.0000	+0.3292
+0.7500	+1.0000	+0.9167	+0.2875
+0.7500	+1.0000	+0.8750	+0.2042
+0.7262	+1.0000	+0.7917	+0.2042
+0.6825	+1.0000	+0.7500	+0.2042
+0.6667	+1.0000	+0.7500	+0.2042
+0.6667	+0.8750	+0.7500	+0.2042
+0.6667	+0.8750	+0.7500	+0.1208
+0.6288	+0.7917	+0.7500	+0.0792
+0.6051	+0.7500	+0.6667	-0.0042
+0.6000	+0.7500	+0.6250	-0.0458
+0.5849	+0.7500	+0.5833	-0.0458
+0.5714	+0.7500	+0.5000	-0.0458
+0.5661	+0.7500	+0.5000	-0.2542
+0.5239	+0.6667	+0.5000	-0.2958
+0.5000	+0.6250	+0.5000	-0.2958
+0.5000	+0.6250	+0.5000	-0.4208
+0.4478	+0.5000	+0.5000	-0.4208
+0.4368	+0.5000	+0.5000	-0.4208
+0.4190	+0.5000	+0.5000	-0.4625
+0.4000	+0.5000	+0.5000	-0.5458
+0.4000	+0.5000	+0.5000	-0.5458
+0.3778	+0.5000	+0.5000	-0.5458
+0.3333	+0.5000	+0.4583	-0.6708
+0.3333	+0.4583	+0.3750	-0.6708
+0.2675	+0.3750	+0.3750	-0.7125
+0.2500	+0.3750	+0.3750	-0.7958
+0.2500	+0.2500	+0.3333	-0.7958
+0.2500	+0.2500	+0.2500	-0.7958
+0.2074	+0.2500	+0.2500	-0.7958
+0.2000	+0.2500	+0.2500	-0.9208

(continues)

T A B L E   4–12 (concluded)

(O-L)/(H-L)	H-C	C-L	C-C
+0.2000	+0.2500	+0.2500	-0.9625
+0.1889	+0.2500	+0.2500	-1.0458
+0.1667	+0.2500	+0.2500	-1.0458
+0.1323	+0.2500	+0.2500	-1.2125
+0.0944	+0.2500	+0.2500	-1.2958
+0.0000	+0.2500	+0.2500	-1.2958
+0.0000	+0.1667	+0.1250	-1.3792
+0.0000	+0.1250	+0.1250	-1.5458
+0.0000	+0.0417	+0.1250	-1.5458
+0.0000	+0.0000	+0.0417	-1.7542
+0.0000	+0.0000	+0.0000	-2.1708
+0.0000	+0.0000	+0.0000	-4.0458

trader's trend method by surprise, although less so than actual prices may have in 1993. Still, more generation of price series might bring in really substantial reaction to the downtrend and possibly even some major uptrends.

The Different Market Price Change Distributions

A word about how and why price series can be markedly different: It comes down to the price change distributions. Though they look similar, (seemingly) slight differences in the close to close price changes found and compared in Tables 4–8, 4–10 and 4–12 for sideways, uptrend, and downtrend markets will make a world of difference (like the difference between making and losing money). Note that the sideways market has extremes of +2.8775 and –1.9558 for its close-to-close changes, and is otherwise evenly spread between plus and minus values, although there are a few more negative cells (27) than positive ones (23), which is offset by larger values in the positive cells.

The uptrend model (Table 4–10), however, has a top cell (higher) value of +4.3609 and a (much smaller) lower value of –.7641, and more plus cells (22) than minus ones (18). The downtrend close-to-close price change distribution table (Table 4–12) has the reverse—a top cell value of only +1.8708 but a bottom one of –4.0458, and far more negative cell values (34) than positive (26).

The degree (number) and extent (size) of the positive and negative cells makes the model produce uptrends (number and sizes of cells swayed to the positive direction) or downtrends (overbalance toward the

Random Walk Model—Generated Prices for Apple Computer (AAPL) from Actual Downtrend Markets

Example #1

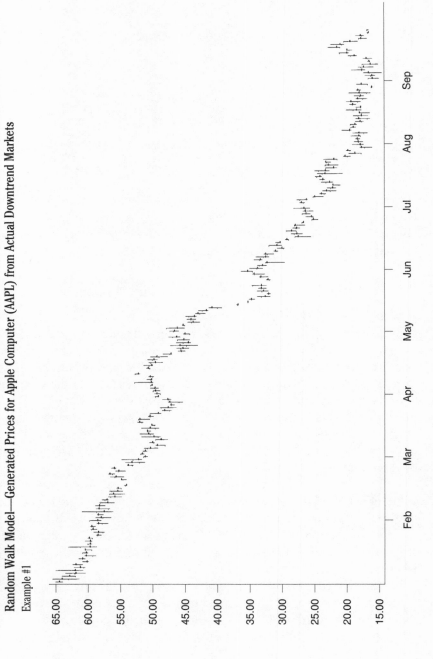

Random Walk Model—Generated Prices for Apple Computer (AAPL) from Actual Downtrend Markets
Example #2

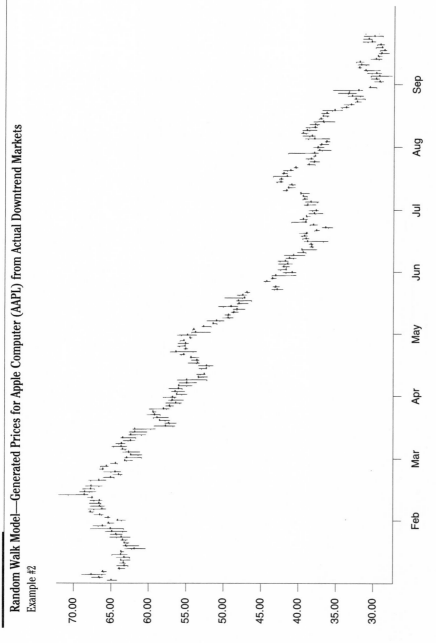

negative side). The more the imbalance in degree and extent, the larger the trend. A perfectly balanced positive/negative distribution will bring about sideways markets, but from time to time good size upmoves and down-moves could occur, even if by computer-chosen random prices; and like-wise for heavily positive or negative distributions—sideways and even significant opposite moves can occur (to forever bedraggle and test the trader's best timing methods).

DIFFERENT MODELS

Turning attention to the second most important ingredient in the data gen-eration equation, the trader must decide which price model to use. The model should match his philosophy on how the markets work and choose from the more academic or more trader-oriented ones. It should also meet standards and evidence market fit.

On the academic side, the model and actual and generated market data should demonstrate that price changes are uncorrelated and that there are no obvious trends or unusual abundance of large price moves, or small trends. For instance, if the stock market headed up from 10 to 100 steadily over the period, even though price changes were uncorrelated (it can happen), the trader might have to refrain from using the random walk model since it assumes no trends are possible (although technically drift can be built into the model by simply having the positive close to close changes much larg-er in size and/or number than the negative ones). Likewise if actual prices rythmically vascillated between 30 and 50, almost on schedule, again even if prices were uncorrelated the trader should probably not use the random walk model. Also, the whole set of close-to-close price changes should fit, or be approximated by, a normal distribution (a Chi-square test can be used to determine closeness of fit). There may be some "lumps" on either end of the price change list—that is, more very large positive or negative ones than the fitness test would normally allow—but if these data are reduced in size or ignored in the test, the test could then come out well. These lumps occur because of unusually large events, price bursts, due to some major event (earnings announcement, government action, etc.).

From a practical standpoint the model should be able to incorporate real and influential events, such as a Gulf War event and its effects on oil prices, and be able to manufacture a like set of price data. So too, for large, slow-trend developments. Also, the model must not just produce unending

124

upward prices but also include some negative (and large in number and size) price moves. Moreover, it should show more "realism" than a walk model: fewer runs (streaks or strings of price changes in the same direction) but runs larger in size, to reflect more sustained and larger influences by investment professionals. Beyond that there is some judgment involved: Do the generated prices of a particular model look real and produce events or drifts that the trader has seen or is looking for as important to represent in the future?

Most important, though, is the trader's philosophy: Does the market act like a large, indecipherable mix of uncontrolled/unknown forces, and thus should he use a random walk or similar model? Or does it act often randomly but also frequently in a more directed, influenced causal manner (e.g., influenced strongly enough by individual traders or groups or governments to cause major price moves/events, or trends, in which case he should choose more deterministic models like the price vector simulator)?

Three Models at Work

To get a feel for how different models generate different or similar prices, we will examine the random walk, sequential walk, and price vector models for one stock.

The stock, Reebok International Ltd, is graphed in Chart 4–28 and covers the period May 1994 through May 1995. The period 5/01/94–4/13/95 will be simulated, as it represents a typical price development for that stock and the market in general (that is, generally uptrend prices growing at about the rate of 15 percent or so per year—from 30 to 35), fairly strong but representative of recent years generally for all stocks. Note that there is still considerable up and down—and sizable at that—price action, not monotonous, unbroken strings of upward price changes.

A note about the generated price charts to follow: They will show months (seemingly real) on the bottom of the chart, but they are just arbitrary dates, needed for the commercial computer program to graph prices. Just think of them as some general period of months in the future.

The Random Walk Model in Action

Table 4–13 tabulates the price change distributions for Reebok for the period in question. Note that there are more positive change cells in the close-to-close price column (column 4), though six are 0 in value—than negative ones, and the top plus value is slightly larger, all of which should

Reebok International, LTD (RBK), 1994–95

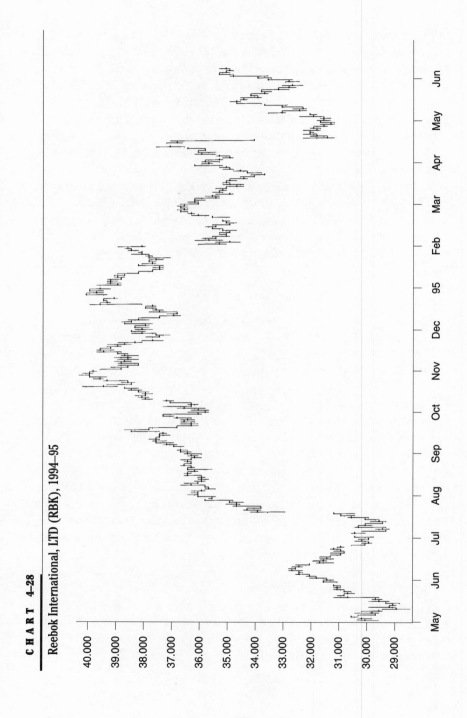

TABLE 4–13

Random Walk Model, Price Change Values; 60 Cells (Values)

Reebok International (RBK) Period: 5/01/94–4/13/95 (Uptrend Market)

(O-L)/(H-L)	H-C	C-L	C-C
+1.0000	+1.0313	+1.1563	+1.7188
+1.0000	+0.8438	+1.0000	+0.9375
+1.0000	+0.7500	+0.8438	+0.7813
+1.0000	+0.7500	+0.7500	+0.7500
+1.0000	+0.6250	+0.6718	+0.6250
+1.0000	+0.6250	+0.6250	+0.5625
+1.0000	+0.5625	+0.6250	+0.5000
+1.0000	+0.5000	+0.5000	+0.5000
+1.0000	+0.5000	+0.5000	+0.4063
+1.0000	+0.5000	+0.5000	+0.3750
+1.0000	+0.5000	+0.5000	+0.3750
+1.0000	+0.5000	+0.5000	+0.3750
+1.0000	+0.4063	+0.5000	+0.3438
+1.0000	+0.3750	+0.5000	+0.2500
+0.8664	+0.3750	+0.3750	+0.2500
+0.8129	+0.3750	+0.3750	+0.2500
+0.7875	+0.3750	+0.3750	+0.2500
+0.7500	+0.3750	+0.3750	+0.2500
+0.7500	+0.3750	+0.3750	+0.2500
+0.7202	+0.3750	+0.3750	+0.2500
+0.6667	+0.3750	+0.3750	+0.1875
+0.6667	+0.2657	+0.3125	+0.1250
+0.6667	+0.2500	+0.2500	+0.1250
+0.6229	+0.2500	+0.2500	+0.1250
+0.5857	+0.2500	+0.2500	+0.1250
+0.5000	+0.2500	+0.2500	+0.1250
+0.5000	+0.2500	+0.2500	+0.1250
+0.5000	+0.2500	+0.2500	+0.1250
+0.5000	+0.2500	+0.2500	+0.0938
+0.4385	+0.2500	+0.2500	+0.0000
+0.3542	+0.2500	+0.2500	+0.0000
+0.3333	+0.2500	+0.2500	+0.0000
+0.3333	+0.1563	+0.2500	+0.0000
+0.3333	+0.1250	+0.2500	+0.0000
+0.3333	+0.1250	+0.1563	+0.0000
+0.3333	+0.1250	+0.1250	-0.1250
+0.3333	+0.1250	+0.1250	-0.1250
+0.3095	+0.1250	+0.1250	-0.1250
+0.2589	+0.1250	+0.1250	-0.1250
+0.2500	+0.1250	+0.1250	-0.1250
+0.2375	+0.1250	+0.1250	-0.1250
+0.2000	+0.1250	+0.1250	-0.1875
+0.2000	+0.1250	+0.1250	-0.2500
+0.1667	+0.1250	+0.1250	-0.2500
+0.1503	+0.1250	+0.1250	-0.2500
+0.1250	+0.1250	+0.1250	-0.2500
+0.0000	+0.0938	+0.1250	-0.2500

(continues)

T A B L E   4–13 (concluded)

(O-L)/(H-L)	H-C	C-L	C-C
+0.0000	+0.0000	+0.0000	-0.3125
+0.0000	+0.0000	+0.0000	-0.3750
+0.0000	+0.0000	+0.0000	-0.3750
+0.0000	+0.0000	+0.0000	-0.3750
+0.0000	+0.0000	+0.0000	-0.3750
+0.0000	+0.0000	+0.0000	-0.5000
+0.0000	+0.0000	+0.0000	-0.5000
+0.0000	+0.0000	+0.0000	-0.5000
+0.0000	+0.0000	+0.0000	-0.6250
+0.0000	+0.0000	+0.0000	-0.6875
+0.0000	+0.0000	+0.0000	-0.9375
+0.0000	+0.0000	+0.0000	-1.5313

explain the generally upward period and hopefully will yield the same for generated data.

Charts 4–29 through 4–31 display three generated price actions for approximately the same period length as the original, real period (Chart 4–28) of Reebok.

The first, Chart 4–29, has the same general result, a move to the 35-plus area, but shows more regular price development, unbroken by significant downside price movement) unlike the original price series. But this conceivably could happen.

The second shows a little more irregular upward price development (some periods of 3 to 4 points downward), but prices grow upwards more, to 50, much more than the real price series. Another possibility: bigger upside trends.

Finally, more realistic price variation is introduced into Chart 4–31 with price counter moves (on the upside) of 3, 4, and 5 points happening almost regularly. But what is happening here? Prices steadily/irregularly move downwards, to close out the period in the 22 area, not the 35 price level experienced by real prices. Whoa! The trader should suspect the model, or, more truthfully, realize that prices in the future could indeed tumble sharply even though he planned on a rising market.

The Sequential Model Applied

Table 4–14 lists price change numbers for Reebook for the period 5/01/94–4/13/95. The relevant (main) price change, close to open, is shown in column 1. It behaves much like that of the close-to-close price

Random Walk Model—Generated Prices for Reebok International (RBK) from Actual Uptrend Prices
Example #1

CHART 4–30

Random Walk Model—Generated Prices for Reebok International (RBK) from Actual Uptrend Prices
Example #2

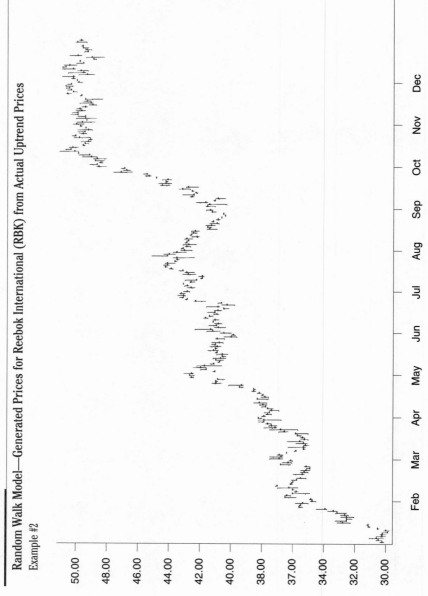

Random Walk Model—Generated Prices for Reebok International (RBK) from Actual Uptrend Prices

Example #3

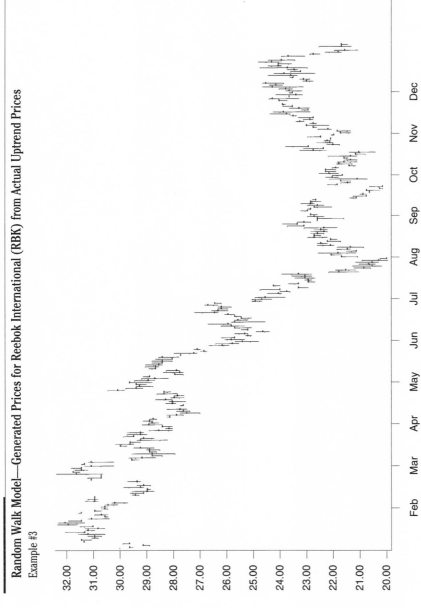

TABLE 4–14

Sequential Walk Model, Price Change Values; 60 Cells (Values)
Reebok International (RBK) Period: 5/01/94–4/13/95 (Uptrend Markets)

O-C	H-O	O-L	(C-L)/(H-L)
+1.1875	+1.4063	+1.0625	+1.0000
+0.3438	+0.9688	+0.8750	+1.0000
+0.2500	+0.8750	+0.7500	+1.0000
+0.2500	+0.8750	+0.7500	+1.0000
+0.2500	+0.7188	+0.6563	+1.0000
+0.2500	+0.6250	+0.6250	+1.0000
+0.2500	+0.6250	+0.6250	+1.0000
+0.2500	+0.6250	+0.5625	+1.0000
+0.2188	+0.6250	+0.5000	+1.0000
+0.1250	+0.5157	+0.5000	+1.0000
+0.1250	+0.5000	+0.5000	+1.0000
+0.1250	+0.5000	+0.5000	+1.0000
+0.1250	+0.5000	+0.4375	+0.9053
+0.1250	+0.4063	+0.3750	+0.8167
+0.1250	+0.3750	+0.3750	+0.8000
+0.1250	+0.3750	+0.3750	+0.8000
+0.1250	+0.3750	+0.3750	+0.7500
+0.1250	+0.3750	+0.3750	+0.7500
+0.1250	+0.3750	+0.3750	+0.7411
+0.0938	+0.3750	+0.3750	+0.6731
+0.0000	+0.3750	+0.2655	+0.6667
+0.0000	+0.3438	+0.2500	+0.6667
+0.0000	+0.2500	+0.2500	+0.6667
+0.0000	+0.2500	+0.2500	+0.6667
+0.0000	+0.2500	+0.2500	+0.6667
+0.0000	+0.2500	+0.2500	+0.6229
+0.0000	+0.2500	+0.2500	+0.5857
+0.0000	+0.2500	+0.2500	+0.5000
+0.0000	+0.2500	+0.2188	+0.5000
+0.0000	+0.2500	+0.1250	+0.5000
+0.0000	+0.2500	+0.1250	+0.5000
+0.0000	+0.2500	+0.1250	+0.5000
+0.0000	+0.2500	+0.1250	+0.5000
+0.0000	+0.2500	+0.1250	+0.5000
+0.0000	+0.1875	+0.1250	+0.4860
+0.0000	+0.1250	+0.1250	+0.4071
+0.0000	+0.1250	+0.1250	+0.3833
+0.0000	+0.1250	+0.1250	+0.3333
+0.0000	+0.1250	+0.1250	+0.3333
-0.0625	+0.1250	+0.1250	+0.3333
-0.1250	+0.1250	+0.1250	+0.3333
-0.1250	+0.1250	+0.1250	+0.3333
-0.1250	+0.1250	+0.1250	+0.2976
-0.1250	+0.1250	+0.1250	+0.2500
-0.1250	+0.1250	+0.1250	+0.2500
-0.1250	+0.1250	+0.1250	+0.2125
-0.1250	+0.0000	+0.1250	+0.1833
-0.1250	+0.0000	+0.0000	+0.1254

(continues)

132

T A B L E   4–14 (concluded)

O-C	H-O	O-L	(C-L)/(H-L)
-0.1250	+0.0000	+0.0000	+0.0000
-0.1250	+0.0000	+0.0000	+0.0000
-0.1250	+0.0000	+0.0000	+0.0000
-0.1563	+0.0000	+0.0000	+0.0000
-0.2500	+0.0000	+0.0000	+0.0000
-0.2500	+0.0000	+0.0000	+0.0000
-0.2500	+0.0000	+0.0000	+0.0000
-0.2500	+0.0000	+0.0000	+0.0000
-0.2500	+0.0000	+0.0000	+0.0000
-0.2500	+0.0000	+0.0000	+0.0000
-0.3750	+0.0000	+0.0000	+0.0000
-0.8125	+0.0000	+0.0000	+0.0000

changes of the random walk model (Table 4–13) in that the numbers of positive changes are larger and the top positive number (+1.1875) is larger than the greatest negative (–.8125), although there are a lot of zero changes nominally made positive.

Charts 4–32 through 4–34 display sequential walk model generated prices for Reebok for a similar period size (about a year). The first, Chart 4–32, grows to an end price a little higher (40) than for the original series (35)—almost double the growth—and has some variation (2 to 3 point drops), but less than the original series (3-, 5-, and even 8-point drops). But still it is a possible, plausible candidate for the future.

Chart 4–33, however, grows much faster, with even less price variation and a larger end price (48 area), more than triple the growth rate of the original series—either a little doubtful to occur, or the avid trend follower can lick his chops for the future!

Finally, a completely different and unbelievable/believable scenario is generated in Chart 4–34. Prices do not grow, they end up at the same price as at the start (at 30), and great price variation (but comparable to that of the original price series) occurs. The trader better hunker down for a long, cold spell of whipping prices!

The Price Vector Model at Work

Table 4–15 lists voluminous statistics that the price vector model needs to generate prices. It requires such data as the number of vector cells for upvectors and their sizes, and the same for downvectors; the greatest number of runs or price change segments in an upvector encountered over the

CHART 4-32

Sequential Walk Model—Generated Prices for Reebok International (RBK) from Actual Uptrend Prices
Example #1

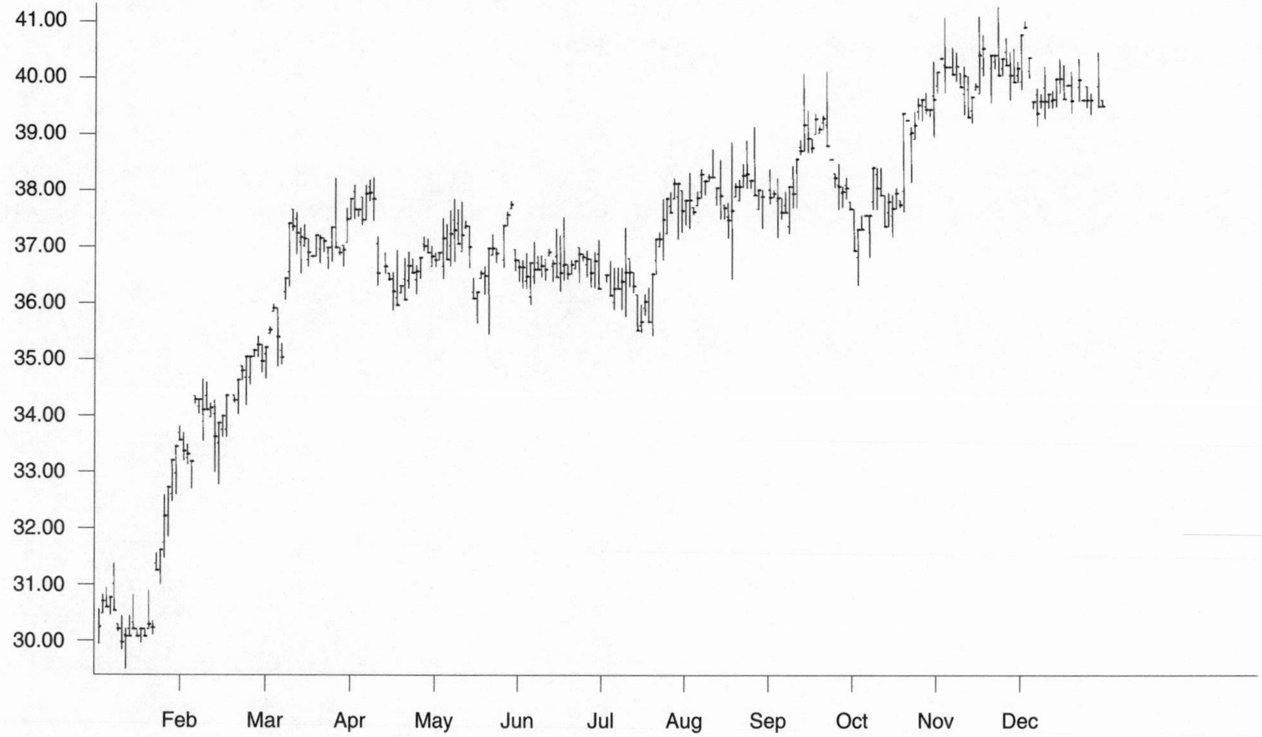

CHART 4-33

Sequential Walk Model—Generated Prices for Reebok International (RBK) from Actual Uptrend Prices

Example #2

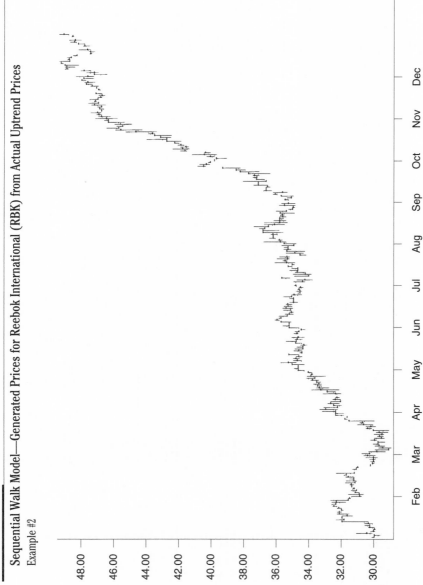

CHART 4-34

Sequential Walk Model—Generated Prices for Reebok International (RBK) from Actual Uptrend Prices
Example #3

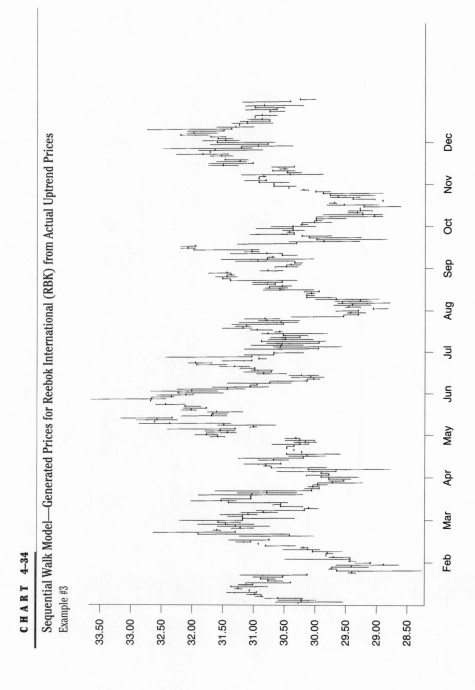

T A B L E   4–15

Simple Price Vector Model, Vector/Cell Information; Vector-Run Random Walk Price Distributions
Reebok International (RBK), 5/01/94–4/13/95

30	5	4	No. vector cells; Max. runs/vector uptrends; Max. runs/vector downtrends
25			No. cell in upvector run #1
12			run #2
8			run #3
6			run #4
2			run #5
30			No. cell in downvector run #1
11			run #2
5			run #3
3			run #4

Upvector runs (ranked)	Downvector runs (ranked)
5.00	4.00
4.00	3.00
4.00	3.00
4.00	3.00
3.00	3.00
3.00	3.00
3.00	3.00
3.00	3.00
3.00	2.00
3.00	2.00
3.00	2.00
3.00	2.00
2.00	2.00
2.00	2.00
2.00	2.00
2.00	2.00
2.00	2.00
2.00	2.00
2.00	2.00
2.00	2.00
2.00	2.00
2.00	2.00
2.00	2.00
2.00	1.00
2.00	1.00
2.00	1.00
1.00	1.00
1.00	1.00
1.00	1.00

(O-L)/(H-L)	H-C	C-L	C-C	
0.7500	0.4375	1.0000	+1.0625	
0.6750	0.3440	0.8750	+0.8125	Upvector run #1
0.5000	0.2500	0.8125	+0.7500	
0.5000	0.2500	0.7500	+0.6875	

(continues)

T A B L E 4–15 (continued)

(O-L)/(H-L)	H-C	C-L	C-C	
0.4771	0.2500	0.6560	+0.6250	
0.3333	0.2500	0.6250	+0.5625	
0.3333	0.2500	0.5625	+0.5000	
0.3333	0.1250	0.5000	+0.3750	
0.2679	0.1250	0.5000	+0.3750	
0.2500	0.1250	0.5000	+0.2500	
0.2250	0.1250	0.5000	+0.2500	
0.2000	0.1250	0.5000	+0.2500	
0.1667	0.1250	0.4375	+0.2500	
0.1458	0.0625	0.3750	+0.2500	
0.1250	0.0000	0.3750	+0.2500	
0.0625	0.0000	0.3750	+0.2500	
0.0000	0.0000	0.2500	+0.1250	
0.0000	0.0000	0.2500	+0.1250	
0.0000	0.0000	0.2500	+0.1250	
0.0000	0.0000	0.2500	+0.1250	
0.0000	0.0000	0.2500	+0.1250	
0.0000	0.0000	0.1250	+0.1250	
0.0000	0.0000	0.1250	+0.1250	
0.0000	0.0000	0.1250	+0.1250	
0.2816	0.2228	0.5163	+0.4837	
0.2816	0.2228	0.5163	+0.4185	
0.2164	0.2228	0.3859	+0.4185	
0.1946	0.2228	0.3859	+0.3533	
0.1946	0.1576	0.3859	+0.3533	
0.1946	0.1576	0.3859	+0.3533	Upvector run #2
0.1946	0.1576	0.3859	+0.3533	
0.1946	0.0924	0.3859	+0.3533	
0.1511	0.0924	0.3859	+0.2880	
0.1511	0.0924	0.3207	+0.2228	
0.1511	0.0924	0.3207	+0.2228	
0.1251	0.0924	0.3207	+0.2228	
0.2267	0.1333	0.4417	+0.5000	
0.1911	0.1333	0.4417	+0.3667	
0.1911	0.0667	0.4417	+0.3667	
0.1911	0.0667	0.4417	+0.3000	
0.1911	0.0667	0.3750	+0.3000	Upvector run #3
0.1911	0.0667	0.3750	+0.3000	
0.1911	0.0667	0.3083	+0.3000	
0.1467	0.0000	0.3083	+0.3000	
0.4545	0.2841	0.4545	+0.4773	
0.4273	0.1477	0.3864	+0.3409	
0.2000	0.1477	0.3864	+0.2727	Upvector run #4
0.2000	0.0795	0.3864	+0.2727	
0.1545	0.0795	0.3864	+0.2727	
0.1273	0.0795	0.3182	+0.2045	
0.5000	0.1250	0.5625	+0.2500	Upvector run #5
0.3125	0.0000	0.0625	+0.1875	

(continues)

138

T A B L E   4–15 (concluded)

(O-L)/(H-L)	H-C	C-L	C-C	
0.7768	0.6750	0.2250	-0.2950	
0.7768	0.6000	0.1500	-0.2950	
0.7768	0.6000	0.1500	-0.2950	
0.7768	0.6000	0.1500	-0.2950	
0.7768	0.6000	0.1500	-0.2950	
0.7768	0.5250	0.1500	-0.2950	
0.7768	0.4500	0.1500	-0.2950	
0.7768	0.3750	0.1500	-0.2950	
0.7768	0.3750	0.1500	-0.2950	
0.7768	0.3750	0.0750	-0.2950	Downvector run #1
0.7768	0.3750	0.0750	-0.2950	
0.7768	0.3750	0.0750	-0.2950	
0.7768	0.3750	0.0750	-0.2950	
0.7768	0.3000	0.0750	-0.2950	
0.7768	0.3000	0.0750	-0.2950	
0.7768	0.3000	0.0750	-0.2950	
0.7768	0.3000	0.0750	-0.3700	
0.7768	0.3000	0.0750	-0.3700	
0.7768	0.3000	0.0750	-0.3700	
0.7768	0.3000	0.0750	-0.3700	
0.6677	0.3000	0.0750	-0.3700	
0.6568	0.3000	0.0750	-0.3700	
0.6568	0.3000	0.0750	-0.3700	
0.6568	0.3000	0.0750	-0.3700	
0.6268	0.3000	0.0750	-0.3700	
0.6268	0.3000	0.0750	-0.3700	
0.6268	0.3000	0.0750	-0.3700	
0.6268	0.2250	0.0750	-0.3700	
0.6268	0.2250	0.0750	-0.3700	
0.6053	0.2250	0.0750	-0.3700	
1.0000	0.7500	0.3750	-0.1250	
1.0000	0.7500	0.2500	-0.1250	
1.0000	0.6250	0.1875	-0.1875	
1.0000	0.6250	0.1250	-0.2500	
1.0000	0.5000	0.1250	-0.3125	
1.0000	0.5000	0.1250	-0.4375	Downvector run #2
1.0000	0.3750	0.1250	-0.5000	
1.0000	0.3750	0.0000	-0.5625	
0.9375	0.2500	0.0000	-0.6250	
0.7619	0.1875	0.0000	-0.9375	
0.2500	0.1250	0.0000	-1.8750	
1.0000	0.6250	0.2500	-0.1875	
1.0000	0.5000	0.1875	-0.3125	
0.8167	0.5000	0.0000	-0.3750	Downvector run #3
0.6190	0.4375	0.0000	-0.4375	
0.2500	0.3125	0.0000	-0.6250	
0.7771	0.4500	0.1500	-0.4000	
0.7771	0.3750	0.1500	-0.4000	Downvector run #4
0.6771	0.3750	0.0750	-0.4000	

real price series' period covered (sampled), and the same for downvectors; the number of cells in typical upvector run/segment number 1—and so on through the longest upvector run number, and the same for downvectors; and finally, random walk price change distribution values (see the headings: close to close [fourth column], high to close, etc.) for both upvectors and downvectors separately, for each typical vector segment.

Charts 4–35 through 4–37 graph three generated price series for the price vector model for about the same period (255 days) as the original price series (242 days). The first, Chart 4–35, ends up almost exactly at the same price as the original price series, at 34. And it experiences both prolonged upward and downward price movements as experienced by the real price series with the same sequence (up first, then down), a close approximation.

The second, Chart 4–36, simply goes nowhere and retains about the same price volatility (up and down price changes) as the original series. This is a possible alternative to a moderately good price net by the original price series. There is also a good deal of randomness built in: Prices do not seem to be able to make concerted (continued) movement in one direction, almost always reversing direction.

Finally, the third graph, Chart 4–37, introduces more reality: both real-life price streaks and net direction. Strings of price moves propel prices in 2 to 3 point upmoves and downmoves with very little resistance or counter price movements (like steps, jumps, or quick drops); see especially the June–September period. But the overall net price change is also a sniff of reality; it may be sobering to a trader expecting a nice net upmove (even a bigger move than experienced in the real price period). Instead he will find a net downmove to 25, a loss of 5 points in Reebok stock. Hopefully his timing method works equally well on downtrends as it does on uptrends!

The next chapter will show how to practically blend elements of portfolio management, ranging from instrument selection, generation of price data for testing purposes, selection and application of timing methods, portfolio simulation, to evaluation and adjustment planning, for a complete trading system.

CHART 4-35

Price Vector Model—Generated Prices for Reebok International (RBK) from Actual Uptrend Prices
Example #1

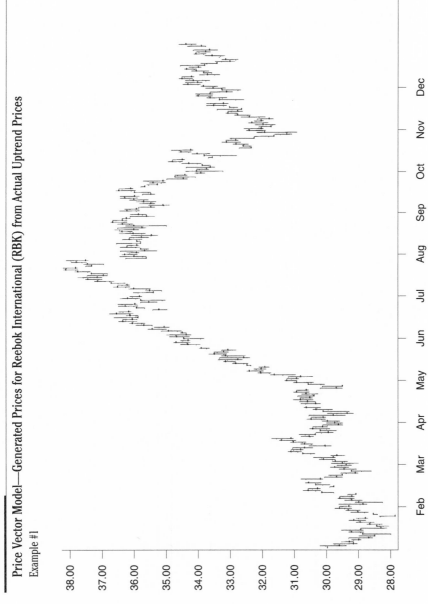

CHART 4-36

Price Vector Model—Generated Prices for Reebok International (RBK) from Actual Uptrend Prices
Example #2

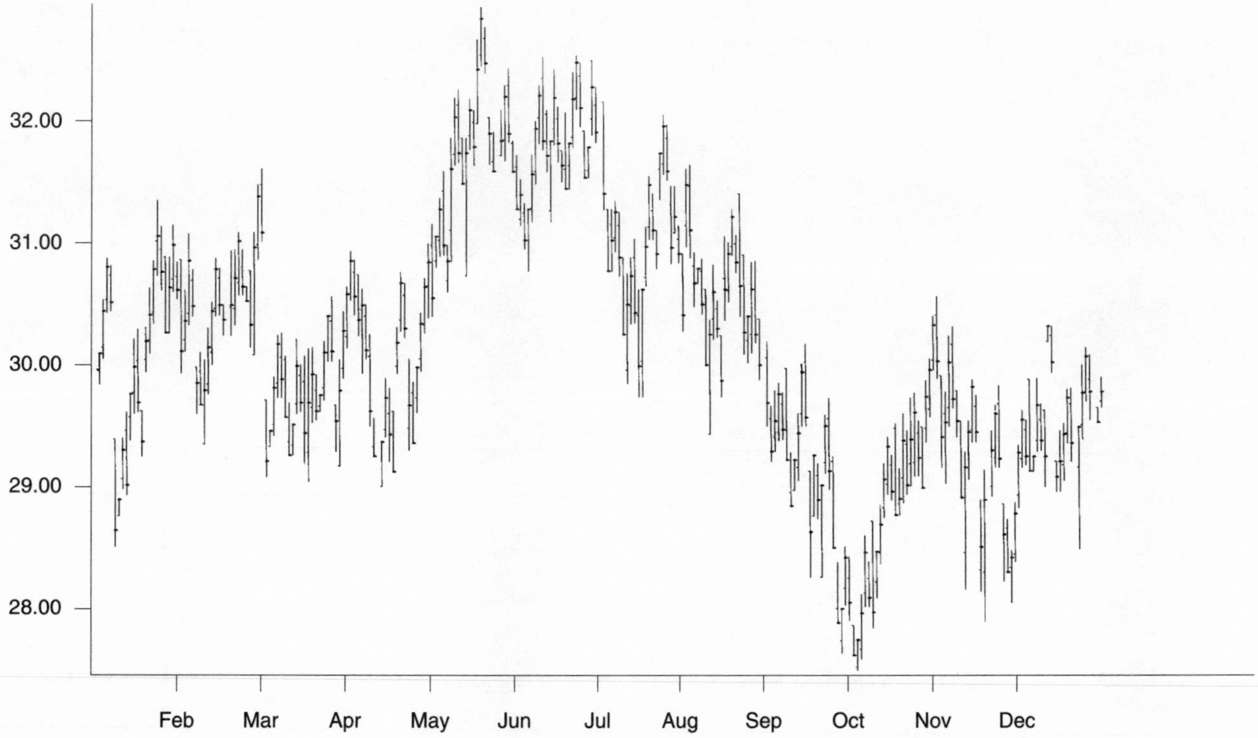

Price Vector Model—Generated Prices for Reebok International (RBK) from Actual Uptrend Prices
Example #3

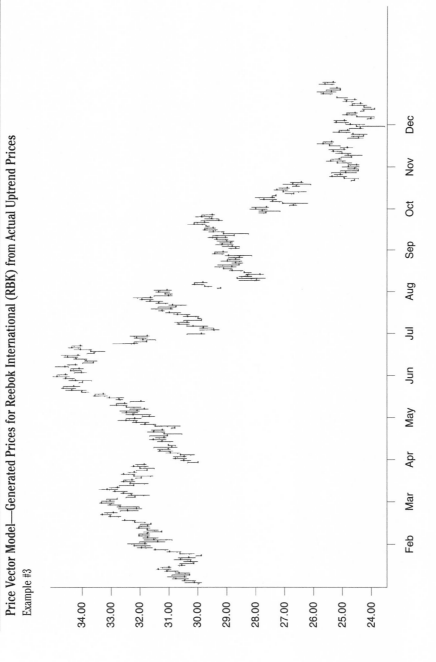

CHAPTER 5

The Complete Trading System

We discussed the overall plan of systematic trading, its components, virtues and do's and don'ts, in Chapter 1.

Risk management—the control of money—was discussed in terms of personal risk evaluations and settings; allocation of monies between investments and reserves and within investments; and evaluating and reengineering elements of risk in the portfolio.

Selecting the best investment candidates was another major topic. The huge panorama of investment opportunities, ranging from low risk/low return government instruments to high risk/high return casino and other chance vehicles was explored. Aspects of return opportunities, volatility, and liquidity of each instrument were discussed.

The third major component, trade timing, an all-important component of the trade system, was very briefly reviewed. The trader could still lose money in his portfolio even with good selection and risk control, if he had poor timing of purchases and sales.

We also reviewed overall portfolio management, setting forth a general plan to incorporate these three areas (risk, selection, and timing) into an operational plan. The plan consisted of managing monies, incorporating trading decisions, and implementing administrative/bookkeeping matters. Above all, it requires discipline, the ability to carry out and stick to the original, overall plan. The details of optimizing and actually implementing this plan, with instructions and numbers, were left for a later time (now!).

In the ensuing chapters we looked at the reasons for investigating trading situations and how simulations (markedly) influence portfolio trading.

Actual trading results were reviewed and found to be greatly lacking. The concept and purpose of simulating and evaluating possible trade results were reviewed. Current approaches, from curve fitting or hindsight to walk-forward, were gone over and found to have shortcomings.

A much more detailed, deeper conceptual insight into trading simulations was put forth in Chapter 3. The concept of simulation, price models in general, and price possibilities were delved into. Price combinations and probabilities of occurrence showed us that there are many (zillions) of price scenarios that our methods have not seen before, and so we need to test and revise our methodologies to prepare for those many possibilities.

This brings us into model test design and, most important, having at our disposal significant numbers and a variety of price scenarios to accurately assess our trading systems' effectiveness for the future.

It turns out the two most important variables are the proper periods of time/types of markets to emulate/reproduce/expand upon for the future and the proper model(s) of price behavior—to make simulated or generated price moves most accurate and representative of future times.

Several more appropriate models were investigated and explained, and examples were given.

Most important, the concept and mechanism for generating or manufacturing price data using past data selection and the aforementioned models were put forth. Many generated price scenario examples of different markets and models were given and discussed.

The final step is to put all these elements together into a working plan to fit each trader.

THE COMPLETE TRADING SYSTEM

The plan consists of two parts that reinforce each other and are continually applied and reviewed: market application and ongoing review/evaluation/research. This means daily operation and periodic review (and possible revision) of parts, or all, of the trading system.

As a practical matter the plan should consist of four parts, depicted in Figure 5–1. They cover aspects of money management—what monies are required and how they should be disbursed or allocated; selection management—the choice of markets and instruments; timing systems

FIGURE 5–1

The Complete Trading System

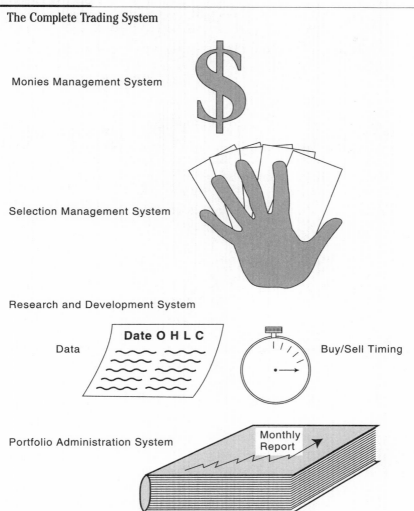

Monies Management System

Selection Management System

Research and Development System

Data   **Date O H L C**   Buy/Sell Timing

Portfolio Administration System   Monthly Report

management—the choices and testing of various purchase/sale mechanisms for individual instruments and market allocations; and portfolio administration management—ranging from daily operation of the whole portfolio to review and evaluation of its performance. In brief, the *what, which, when,* and *how* of investment management.

All parts of the plan work together as an integrated/related whole entity. If one breaks down (say, the timing programs; poor timing mounts up losses in individual trades, and thus the whole portfolio and its performance suffers and steps may have to be taken to correct the problem), the whole system suffers.

THE MONIES MANAGEMENT SYSTEM

Basically the monies management part of the entire system is concerned with assessing/categorizing investment alternatives and their risk, matching the trader with investments that meet his risk tolerance as a whole, then allocating capital initially and reallocating as the portfolio grows or shrinks, according to a schedule or plan he has set up.

Figure 5–2 breaks down the monies management system, the (*what*) monies part of the whole system, into its components.

Return/Risk Categorization and Assignment

The first part concerns categorizing different risk alternatives and matching the appropriate ones to the trader's portfolio.

The trader must look deep inside himself. Is he really a speculator, willing to lose one-half or more of his capital for a chance to double his account or better? Or does he avoid even moderate losses of 10 to 20 percent of his capital? Most traders are probably in between—they want a good deal of growth and are willing and able psychologically and monetarily to undertake such a commitment.

Later on he will use either a Sharpe ratio, drawdown statistic, or a new one—the gain/pain index, to evaluate and adjust his portfolio. He should strive to live with one of these or come up with a risk/return measure that he understands and accepts and use it continually and without equivocation. So he must look in the mirror and see the truth—whether he is conservative or speculative, and to what degree.

Once he has assessed himself for investment perspective, he can list, sort, and choose the instruments appropriate for that outlook. If he were very conservative, he should choose low-risk investments (albeit low returns come with this choice; it is inevitable—there is no free lunch) such as government bonds, where the full faith and credit and resources of the central government are behind them. A little more risky and harder to liquidate or control are foreign government bonds, especially those linked to shaky or new regimes.

FIGURE 5–2

The Monies Management System

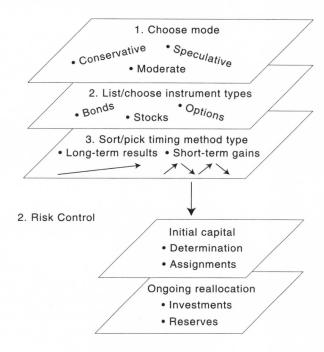

1. Risk/Return Categorization/Assignment

1. Choose mode
• Conservative   • Speculative
• Moderate

2. List/choose instrument types
• Bonds   • Stocks   • Options

3. Sort/pick timing method type
• Long-term results   • Short-term gains

2. Risk Control

Initial capital
• Determination
• Assignments

Ongoing reallocation
• Investments
• Reserves

In the other extreme, if losses were not disastrous (would not wipe out the account) and he could indeed stand large relative losses or losing periods (even small cumulative losses over a long, long time bother some traders, more than the losses themselves), and the chance (even small) of making a great deal of money is so important to him, the trader could choose instruments that had high potential gains and go for it.

Another possibility, especially if the trader were somewhere in between the risk-taking type and the risk-averse type, is to include midrisk and midreturn instruments in his portfolio. Examples of these are stocks, some commodities such as S&P futures, which simulate the whole market and therefore average out individual stock risk and return, and interest rate futures, which are a hedge or bet on the main driving engine for many instruments. Others include corporate convertible bonds, which are a combination and hedge on more conservative bond returns and less risk; to the convertible feature of the bond, which allows the investor to change his bond investment into a stock (or he can simply retain the bond, as its price will reflect stock rises/falls in the stock itself).

The investor can hedge or position himself a little more toward the middle, or toward either extreme, by simply placing some—a small portion—of his investment in that area. Typically this portion amounts to 10–20 percent of the capital invested. Another strategy, which we will address more in depth later, is to distribute or allocate his funds amongst many instruments. This acts to reduce risk and is used to guard against big individual losses, especially in risky instruments.

Note that we are assigning/choosing certain categories or types of investments to participate in, but not choosing the actual individual instruments. We are interested here in the degree or general risk influence of instrument categories. We will choose individual items in each selected category later on.

The next step is to consider and choose one or more timing methods that fit the risk modes chosen. We are not choosing a particular one to use exclusively at this time (later we will apply and choose them based on their effectiveness in research tests), but rather selecting *types* of approaches that fit our trader's risk categorization. For example, moving averages have the capability of being set to follow long-term trends and should be included in a risk-averting or lower-risk program, whereas oscillators probably should not be considered for this risk outlook since they are so sensitive to price action and tend to take new investment postures prematurely, far before a new price direction is certain.

Risk Control

Once risk mode, instrument types, and timing methods have been categorized and assigned for the trader's portfolio, he must address the monies control aspect of the system. The second part of Figure 5–2 lists the main components: initial and ongoing capital allocation.

Initial capital allocation can be a little tricky. How much to start with is determined first, but capital is not specifically assigned to various instruments like Boeing stock or cattle futures at this time. Rather, the numbers of money assignments, and how much for each, are calculated. Later on we will assign specific monies to each instrument.

The core of this process is to tie the degree of risk aversion to the amount of money needed to withstand future loss periods, indeed for the life of the investment. And it is hard to know exactly what losing periods there are going to be, or that are even probable. They are dependent upon which instruments are selected, how much monies are placed in each, and the future price history of each instrument. The trader doesn't know exactly what will happen to his stocks (or whatever), so how can he plan on what losses to expect? Fortunately, as we discussed in detail in Chapter 4, the trader can come up with many representative price scenarios, and hence the more probable portfolio values, if he does a rigorous set of simulations (as described in that chapter).

Determining Initial Capital

The determination/calculation of the initial capital requirement for the trader's account starts with the determination by the trader of the maximum dollar loss he will tolerate (call it maxloss), and then with a choice of certainty or probability of loss in the account (call it probloss). The lower the value of probloss, the less likely he will lose the money (maxloss). Typically, statisticians use values ranging from 10 percent down to as low as 0.1 percent, a very unlikely event. A frisky trader will opt for 10 percent, that is, a probability of 10 percent over the life of the account that he will lose as much as maxloss (his loss kitty, or point at which he will quit trading the portfolio), or as much as that from subsequent high points or peaks in the account.

As we will see in the administration section, the latter situation (peak-to-trough loss period of maxloss) is more of a wake-up call for a temporary hold or serious reassessment of the account, whereas the former is a survival number meant to ensure that the account weathers the very first investment storm. For instance, an individual, fairly conservative trader might choose 1 percent as his probloss and $50,000 as his maxloss, the money he is willing to swallow in this investment undertaking. A more frisky speculative trader might choose 10 percent as his probloss, and $100,000 as his maxloss.

Calculating Number of Instruments

Once his maxloss and probloss numbers have been chosen, the next thing to determine is the maximum number of instruments to be selected for portfolio inclusion. As mentioned before, it is to the trader's advantage to diversify as much as possible, but only to the point where new instrument additions start showing return potential less than the average of the current instruments chosen for the portfolio.

If possible, the trader should include a minimum of 10 instruments to let diversification really start to work. Also, within the instruments selected, instruments having the highest return and the same general risk/loss potential as others for the timing methods used and the projected price action (see simulation of generated data, Chapter 4) should be chosen.

Having more than 100 distinct, different instruments in the portfolio does not materially reduce risk any further either. For administrative purposes it is also harder to keep track of more than that number. A choice of more than 100 would be appropriate only for liquidity purposes, to allow additional or large amounts of capital to be allocated.

It is also more advantageous (mathematically speaking) to allocate evenly across all instruments, both initially and with increases in capital in the account at a later point in time, whether due to additions to or gains in the portfolio.

The question of reserve monies versus capital investment in instruments is important but can only be answered by portfolio simulations. See the section on timing and portfolio management, later. In it we propose what portion—a fixed percent throughout the simulation period—of assets are invested, the balance in cash or equivalent reserves. Typically the reserves are as low as 50 percent—for speculative traders—to as high as 90 percent for conservative, risk-conscious investors, such as those acting as funds and pension management. Most often the invested assets are leveraged with margin (borrowed) monies, from as little as 1 cent or even less required (e.g., with cash currencies) to purchase or sell short 1 dollar's worth of assets, to as much as 50 cents needed (e.g., for stocks). Again, the cash reserves versus instrument investments are calculated in the portfolio simulation, to follow.

THE SELECTION MANAGEMENT SYSTEM

Per the prior section the trader has selected area(s) of risk that reflect his investment stance and/or monies available and has made a first cut at allocating initial monies to those repective areas. The only way he can accurately gauge whether that first cut or subsequent revisits/refinements of that choice are valid and satisfactory for his overall risk mode is to simulate that specific mix, selected instruments and timing programs in a portfolio simulation program, which puts it all together and reports probable and most-likely profit outcomes for the future.

The selection process is also an initial and ongoing/reiterative process whereby different markets and instruments are considered for inclusion in the portfolio simulations, and if successful put into the actual portfolio, and later on reevaluated.

All markets are considered, those that meet maximum risk or fewer requirements appropriate for the trader are then considered and individual instruments within that category are then examined. See Figure 5–3. For example, if his risk stance turns out to be moderate, he would only consider moderate- to-low-risk investments such as stocks (but not all—some are quite risky, more than the moderate risk he required), bonds, and cash equivalents (CDs, etc.).

Within each acceptable market individual instruments are then examined. Each one or group (he could group like commodities, such as grains, together, if their price action is highly correlated each to the others) must

F I G U R E   5–3

The Selection Management System

Markets . . .

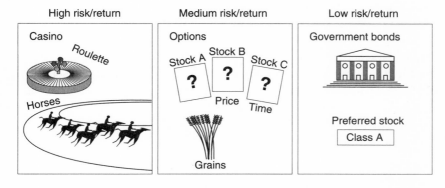

Individual Investments. . .

Stocks
. . . Boeing?
. . . AT&T?
. . . Intel?
. . . Netscape?
. . . FUNN?

also pass the maximum risk filter individually or as a basket (some low, some moderate, some high risk, but averaging to no more than the maximum dollar risk allowed in his portfolio). Again, risk is measured as a maximum dollar cumulative loss (maxloss) over a period of time with a specified probability of occurring (probloss). The actual numbers for each instrument or the portfolio as a conglomerate of many instruments are gathered from the portfolio and/or individual instrument performances simulation over some projected period of time (to be discussed later).

For example, the moderate risk trader would probably consider the broad stock category. He could (theoretically) consider the entire list of all exchanges, including the NASDAQ, and separately look at securities ranging from low-risk giants like AT&T on the NYSE to tiny entertainment stocks like FUNN on the NASDAQ and individually accept or reject them for portfolio candidacy. Or he could elect to consider placing $x total for certain higher-maximum-loss–estimated stocks as a group, and the same for lower-risk groups that included AT&T. The two groups would balance each other and average to the moderate risk the trader wanted in the first place. This is a natural carryover to market segments—like airlines, chemicals, computer software, and so forth—which act alike within groups. It is still best to vary some stock characteristics like risk amongst groups, to avoid performances that are too similar and defeat the purpose of diversification.

Some use price correlation tests between a stock and a group, or between two groups, to further ensure some (as much as possible) degree of independence. This is also a way of seeking diversification: a reading of close to 1.0 or even as high as 0.3 or 0.4 indicates a good deal of close relationship or similar price movements between stocks or groups, which is what he is trying to avoid. What he really wants is a reading of 0.0 to 0.2 or so, in which case he would then put those tested (pairs of) stocks in the portfolio.

THE RESEARCH AND DEVELOPMENT SYSTEM

Research and testing are the end points, the culmination of setting risk controls and selecting trading instruments. It is here that the trader sets up or hypothecates some possible portfolios, then tests for and evaluates expected performance. If the evaluation comes up wanting (i.e., the profit performance is not satisfactory), he will go back and readjust/propose a new portfolio. When it is satisfactory, he turns the research methodology into real-time operational trading by concentrating on portfolio administration (discussed later).

Figure 5–4 outlines the research and development system. We have discussed most elements before: timing methods and risk aspects of the portfolio were discussed in Chapter 1; instrument selection was reviewed in that chapter and in this one; and the creation and use of generated price

FIGURE 5–4

The Research and Development System

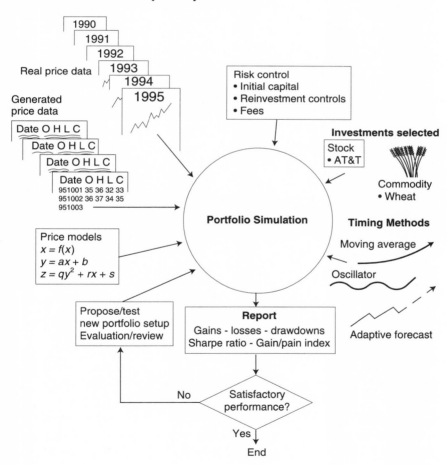

data, actual price data, and price models were thoroughly discussed in Chapter 4. Now it is time to put all these components together in a workable research and development package to be used in real-time trading!

First, he must line up the investment types he selected (see selection management section, this chapter). Next, risk control numbers (initial capital and fee charges) and control factors (reinvestment algorithm or scheme) must be set up (see monies management section, this chapter).

The newest element (and a very important one) in the cauldron of research is the price data, the all-important application/testing area for the timing models. A true research area and trader decision function, generating price data involves identifying and utilizing historical data from selected instruments as input to generated data, which will in turn be tested by the timing methods.

Trade timing mechanisms or methods must next be brought in so that he can find out and maximize the profit or loss performance on each instrument for hypothesized (future) periods of time. The output of these timing tests will be used directly in the portfolio simulation.

Finally, the results of trade timing and specified risk control parameters set up by the trader are used as input to a portfolio simulation program. This program basically simulates or mimics the actions of a trader and his methods in the marketplace and produces profit/loss and other measures of performance. A typical output was shown in Table 2–1, Chapter 2.

Several main portfolio simulation output statistics were discussed (add the Gain/Pain Index—see Chapter 1) and a five-year period of simulated trading with specially selected S & P 500 stocks was presented. Especially important statistics are net gains, average drawdown and/or Sharpe ratio, and the Gain/Pain Index; and secondarily, profit per trade (to be studied/improved in case costs are higher than thought—a low figure could mean marginal or no profits with higher costs of trading) and time per trade (the total time in trading may be smaller than total time available and thus provide the trader with freed time for extra trades elsewhere and mean more total profits).

THE PORTFOLIO ADMINISTRATION SYSTEM

This system is the culmination of the research and development spadework done by the trader and represents the final stage: real-time trading. Here is the payoff for all the investigation into risk monies required, risk controls, what instruments to select, timing methods to use, settings to use to optimize those methods, and performance results to expect and serve as guidelines for monitoring real time results.

Figure 5–5 details the components of the last, but most important system, the in-market administration of the portfolio.

F I G U R E   5–5

The Portfolio Administration System

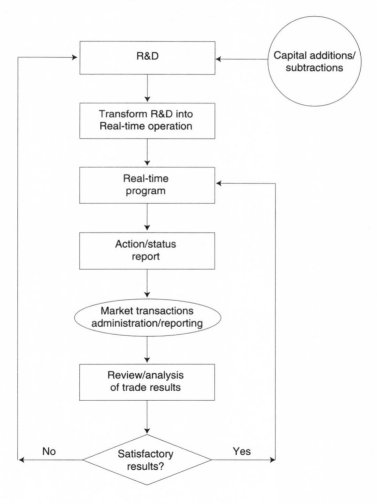

All the fruits of the R&D effort must be first transformed into workable daily or other periodic use. Research and development is the engine, the source of power, the architecture of trading; it specifies capital allocation, instrument selection, and purchase and sale timing of trades. The real-time operation consists of transforming all the research into simplified, efficient, workable use for the actual marketplace.

Initially the trader will have specified risk parameters, such as initial capital he has determined; instruments selected; and timing methods chosen. Then he will run the research programs and come up with satisfactory portfolio results, all detailed in the previous section.

The major task of the trader, now putting on his administrative cap, is to translate or transform the research system into a workable/usable program for the real-time, actual markets. This involves taking his research program for timing buying and selling, and changing it into a daily action and status reporting mechanism, which in turn will produce an action/status report such as shown in Table 1–2 in Chapter 1. In it he will calculate and display buy and sell prices for each instrument, as well as keep track of where each instrument stands at each point in time.

This report will be used for trading his portfolio on a daily, weekly, or whatever time basis he has chosen, the next and central step in the process. In addition to transaction of market orders, he will have to keep track, in a bookkeeping sense, of all the transactions. The administrative matters consist primarily of confirmations, results of transactions, and periodic status reports (often on a daily, but at least monthly basis).

Next, he will wish to review the progress of the portfolio and perhaps report to others (shareholders/partners and/or regulatory bodies) the status of the portfolio.

If the results are essentially on track, well within the bounds allowed or called for by the research and development studies (actual profits, drawdown statistics, etc., are analyzed to see if they are within reasonable range of projected figures), then he continues running the in-market trading program as is.

If they are not satisfactory (profits are half or less of what was expected, or they are negative; a drawdown is far larger than the worst projected; or the average drawdown is twice as large as anticipated, etc.), then he must return to the research and development system to discover why they are unsatisfactory and correct the situation. He must then propose ways to improve the performance (e.g., new timing methods, different settings on the methods, more capital to withstand unanticipated market periods) and retest those solutions in the portfolio simulation. When a satisfactory simulation result has been attained he can then transform changes into the in-market program (e.g., addition of a new timing program or changed settings in the current timing programs) and institute that changed program into real-time trading operations.

If he has not found satisfactory solutions to the poorer performance situation, the trader must decide whether to accept those inferior results for the future or to halt trading until a satisfactory portfolio trading system can be found.

Finally, there may be additions or subtractions of capital to the portfolio. These changes must be run through the research and development system (unless provisions have already been made to incorporate capital changes ongoing) to see the effect of capital changes to the overall portfolio performance. He would like to know if adding money at times of significant portfolio value surges or drops will have immediate or long-term effects on the portfolio: Is it better to add on major pullbacks? Do portfolio peaks mean exaggerated losses for new monies soon thereafter? Hopefully the trader has determined beforehand, through exhaustive portfolio what-if, capital infusion scenarios, that timing of these infusions is immaterial in the long run, so that he can simply add monies to his portfolio and put them to work any time. Sometimes, though, big runups in a portfolio reflect major trends and soon to be major reactions, which might mean more certain and significant losses for new trades and new monies.

SUMMARY/EXAMPLES

We discussed the complete trading system, all the components needed to put together a successful trading operation. Each subsystem—monies management, instrument selection management, research and development, and portfolio administration—was outlined and discussed. Details and examples of each were discussed in previous chapters. In this chapter we concentrated on the general workings of each, the relationships between them, and how they work together as one entity.

The following set of procedures is a compact version of the workings, examples and interrelationships of the four subsystems, and the trading system as a whole. For details and explanations and in-depth discussion, refer to the appropriate sections in this chapter.

The Complete Trading System

I. The Monies Management System
  A. Risk/return categorization and assignment
    1. Choose return/risk mode (e.g., conservative, moderate, speculative)
    2. List and choose market instrument areas (e.g., bonds, stocks, commodities) to match the return/risk mode selected
    3. List and choose timing methods (e.g., moving averages, oscillators, RSI) to match the return/risk mode chosen
  B. Risk controls set up
    1. Determine initial capital requirements (e.g., $50,000 for speculative trader)
    2. Determine number of instruments (e.g., 15 tradeable instruments)
    3. Assign capital amounts to instrument types (e.g., $30,000 to commodities)
    4. Determine invested and reserve capital amounts (e.g., $50,000 invested; $50,000 reserves)

II. The Selection Management System
  A. Choose individual markets per risk mode (e.g., interest rate futures for a conservative trader).
    This is a refinement of I.A.2, choose market types
  B. Choose individual instruments (e.g., T-bond, Eurodollar, T-bill futures per II.A selection example)

III. The Research and Development System
  A. Gather risk control specifications (see I.A and I.B for risk mode and market types choices)
  B. Gather market and individual instrument selections (see II.A and II.B choices)
  C. Choose price models (e.g., sequential walk model)
  D. Choose time periods for instruments selected (e.g., 1987 for various stocks, 1995 for others)
  E. Gather price data for instruments and timing periods selected (e.g., daily basis price data for 1987 Boeing stock)

F. Generate sufficient numbers of future price scenarios (e.g., 100 separate years for Boeing stock based on 1987 prices, and another 100 years for Boeing based on 1992 prices)

G. Test timing methods on generated price scenarios (e.g., moving average tests on data developed in III.F)

H. Choose optimum test settings for methods and instruments tested (e.g., 5 and 20 moving average worked best [maximum profit, smallest average drawdown, or highest Sharpe or Gain/Pain Index] for Boeing stock)

I. Run portfolio simulation on best methods for each instrument (e.g., mix together best moving average setting for Boeing and do the same separately for other stocks, then similarly for other methods, until a matrix of methods/instruments has been put together)

J. Evaluate portfolio performances (e.g., profit per year of 15.8 percent; average drawdown of 3.5 percent; Sharpe ratio monthly was 0.42; Gain/Pain Index calculated to +34.3)

K. Research analysis: if satisfactory performance, continue to IV; if not, return to I (e.g., remove contrary bands method, substitute vulume–price breakout timing method, and increase initial capital to $200,000 from $100,000)

IV. The Portfolio Administration System

A. Transform research and development system into real time with action/status reporting (e.g., moving average timing program action—taking prices and current instrument status—see Table 1–2)

B. Run real-time trading programs (on a daily or whatever basis)

C. Administrate trading (e.g., periodic confirms, status reports to partners and regulatory agencies)

D. Review/analyze trade results (e.g., monitor profit/loss monthly to see if returns are annualizing to 15.8 percent; drawdowns not more than 11.5 percent)

E. If unsatisfactory results, return to III (e.g., profits at year end are –3.2 percent; or largest drawdown is 16.4 percent compared with 11.2 percent in research and development testing) If satisfactory results, continue to IV.B

INDEX

A

Adaptive forecast, 10
Amdahl Corp.
  price vector model, 87–89
  prices, 82
  random walk model, 83–85
  sequential walk model, 86
Apple Computer
  downtrend market, 94, 111, 114,
    120–123
  sideways market, 92, 95–111
  uptrend market, 93, 111–119
Approximation, 56

B

Box size breakout, 10
Brokers, selecting a, 12

C

Calmar ratio, 3, 4
Candidate selection, 7–9, 45
Candlestick theory, 42
Cash investment needs, 11
Cash reserve, 11
Chart formations, 10
Charting, 26, 42, 58
Chi-square test, 124
Commodity Profits through Trend Trading,
  64
Complete trading system, 145–161
  list of procedures, 160, 161
  monies management system, 148–152
  portfolio administration system, 156–159
  research and development system,
    154–156
  selection management system, 152–154
Contrary, 10
Contrary bands, 10

Correlation tests, 154
Curve fitting/hindsight, 23

D

Daily operational control, 12–14
Deterministic, 56
Discipline habits, 14–17
Diversification, 8, 45
Dow theory, 42, 43
Downtrend markets, 94, 111, 114, 120–123
Drawdown statistic, 5, 6

E

Elliot wave, 10, 42

F

Forecast, 10
Fundamental, 10

G

Gain/pain index, 6, 7
General price theories, 42
Geometric mean, 4

I

Implementation of plan; *see* Complete
  trading system
Individual risk outlook, 2
Initial and reinvestment monies, 11, 12
Initial capital, 11, 151
Instrument selection, 7–9, 45, 151, 152
Investment speedometer, 7, 8

J

Japanese yen - continuous contract
  price vector model, 77–81
  prices, 71

Japanese yen - continuous contract,
continued
random walk model, 72–75
sequential walk model, 76
Jones, Deane, 4

L

Leverage, 152
LINK flight simulator, 33

M

Managed account industry, 22, 23
Management discipline, 14–17
Market allocation, 7, 8
Measuring risk, 2–7
Midrisk/midreturn instruments, 149
Minimal prediction school of price model,
57, 58
Minimum cash amount, 11
Mixed model of price movement, 35, 36
Moderate risk trader, 154
Monies management system, 148–152, 160
Moving average, 10, 45

O

Operational trading program, 12–14
Operations research, 26
Orderedness, 4
Overall portfolio plan; *see* Complete trad-
ing system

P

Pattern decision, 10
Perfection, 56
Personal risk attitude, 2
Portfolio administration system, 156–159,
161
Portfolio management, 11–17
Price behavior, 33–46
magnitude of change, 40, 41
order/sequence, 40, 41
price models, 42, 43
reducing number of price scenarios,
43–45

Price behavior, *continued*
scenario possibilities, 36–40, 43
schools of thought, 34–36
trend moves, 40, 42
Price change distributions, 121, 124
Price model schools, 57, 58
Price models, 42, 43, 56–58
Price paths, 37–40
Price scenario generation, 47–143
downtrend markets, 94, 111, 114,
120–123
generation of price data, 89–91
main elements, 47
past period selection, 47–49
period size, 49
price change distributions, 121, 124
price characteristics, 49–56
price model selection, 56–58, 124, 125
price vector model; *see* Price vector
model
random walk model; *see* Random walk
model
sequential walk model; *see* Sequential
walk model
sideways markets, 91–111
subevents, 50
time considerations, 49
uptrend markets, 93, 111–119
Price vector model
data collection, 66–68
examples
Amdahl Corp., 87–89
Japanese yen - continuous contract,
77–81
Reebok International, 133, 137–143
model description, 64–66, 77
price construction procedures, 68–70
Probabilistic, 56, 58
Profit per trade, 156

R

Random walk model
downtrend markets, and, 111, 114,
120–123

Random walk model, *continued*
  examples
    Amdahl Corp., 83–85
    Japanese yen - continuous contract, 72–75
    Reebok International, 125–131
  model description, 58–62
  sideways markets, and, 95–111
  uptrend markets, and, 111–119
Random walk theorists, 35, 36
Real-time results, 21–23
Reebok International
  price vector model, 133, 137–143
  random walk model, 125–131
  sequential walk model, 128, 132–136
Related events school of price models, 57, 58
Relative strength, 10
Research and development system, 154–156, 160, 161
Reserve monies, 11, 152
Return-and-risk analysis portfolio tuning, 45, 46
Risk, measuring, 2–7, 148, 149
Risk attitude, 2
Risk control, 150–152, 160

S

Selection management system, 152–154, 160
Selection of trading candidates, 7–9, 45
Sequential walk model
  examples
    Amdahl Corp., 86
    Japanese yen - future contract, 76
    Reebok International, 128, 132–136
  model description, 62, 63
Sharpe, William, 2
Sharpe ratio, 2, 3, 6
Sideways markets, 91–111
Simulations, 19–31
  barometer statistics, 27
  general workings, 30
  good simulations, bad results, 20, 21

Simulations, *continued*
  measures of performance, 27–31
  nature of, 26
  origin, 26
  output lists, 28–31
  purpose, 30
  real-time results, 21–23
  testing approaches, 23–26
  uses, 27
Sinusoidal waves, 42
Special statistic/event school of price models, 57, 58
Sterling ratio, 4
Strong condition, 48
Switching device, 8
Systematic trading, 1–17
  portfolio management, 11–17
  risk management, 1–7
  selection of trading candidates, 7–9
  timing methods, 9, 10

T

Time per trade, 156
Timing methods, 9, 10, 45
Trading simulations; *see* Simulations
Trading timing, 9, 10, 45
Trend, 10
Trend school of price movement, 34, 35
Types of price scenarios, 50–56

U

Uptrend markets, 93, 111–119

V

Vince, Ralph, 4

W

Walk forward, 25
Weak case, 48
Whipsaw markets, 40

Y

Young, Terry, 3

Other books of interest by Robert M. Barnes:

High-Impact Day Trading

This best-seller examines several popular day trading techniques;
straightforward, sophisticated, and filled with easy-to-follow examples.
ISBN: 0-7863-0798-6

Trading in Choppy Markets

Renowned trader Robert Barnes analyzes the markets and develops
methods for the most common choppy market situations; also covers
20 popular and proven trading methods.
ISBN: 0-7863-1007-3